GARY YANKER'S

WALKING WORKOUTS

Runners, dancers, bodybuilders, racquet sports players, bicyclists, swimmers, and skiers—learn how to make walking work for you indoors, outdoors, all year round—whenever and wherever it's best for you. Learn how to avoid shin splints and hamstring pulls . . . how to increase strength and endurance by weight-loaded walking.

Gary Yanker shows how walking can transform your body *and* your life. It's all here . . . in a simple, safe, effective regimen that can bring you lifelong pleasure. All you need are your own two legs—and get-up-and-go!

Gary Yanker has been dubbed America's foremost walking expert by the *Miami Herald* and NBC's *Today Show,* and is generally considered the guru of the walking movement. Since giving up the full-time practice of law four years ago, he has devoted his life to making walking the number one exercise in America. Gary Yanker is the founding editor of *Walking World* magazine.

GARY YANKER'S

WALKING

How to Use Your Walking Body as the Ultimate Exercise Machine

WORKOUTS

by Gary Yanker

PHOTOGRAPHY BY
MICHAEL BENNETT

WARNER BOOKS
A Warner Communications Company

A Warner Communications Company

Library of Congress Cataloging in Publication Data

Yanker, Gary
   Gary Yanker's Walking workouts.

      1. Walking. 2. Physical fitness. I. Title.
II. Title: Walking workouts.
GV199.5.Y363   1985   613.7′1   85-10550
ISBN 0-446-39109-3 (U.S.A.)
      0-446-39110-7 (Can.)

Book design by Paula Schlosser
Produced by Helene Siegel

Printed in the United States of America

First Printing: November 1985

10   9   8   7   6   5

To my father, Pete Yanker, who believes
you don't have to be a "winner" at a sport,
but just love doing it.

ACKNOWLEDGMENTS

I WISH TO THANK the following people for their assistance:

Tom and Dina Orr of the 21st Century Nautilus Training and Testing Center for providing their members, facilities, trainers and physical fitness consultants to help with the Workouts, in particular, Eda Martin, Ross Jacobs and Cecilia Houseman, Kelly Kane (exercise models), Leslie Altman (stretching consultant), Gregory Blake (aerobics consultant), Andy Bostinto (weight trainer), Jim Breslin (sports training), Frank Maggi, and Terry Cohen.

Patti Breitman, Carol Tarlow, Theresa Dziorney, Virginia Rice, Michael Bennett, Betsy Livingston, Dr. Alan Selner, Alfredo Santana, Nancy McCord, Shirley R. Davis, Jennifer Romine, Carol Spina, Jerry Gorman, Linda Cassens, David Clow, Diana Adams, Toni Tenille, Bob Defer, Ron Laird, Timothy R. Quinn, Richard S. Polk, Ben Sackheim, Paula Panich, Jody Lewis, Neil Finn, Ginna Rogers Gould, Jean Mac-Guire, T. George Harris for their advice, research and editorial support; the staff of Warner Books, *American Health*, *Walking World*, Quality International and The Rockport Shoe Company.

Special thanks to my advisors and supporters of walking throughout the world: In the U.S.: Lynn O'Rourke Hayes, Jens Bang, Jody Weiss, Drew Mearns, Mitch Douglas, Jerry Petitt, Jerry Bynum, Laura Alvord, Carrie Corbin, Laura Martin, Donna Adkins, Peg Sinclair, Sandi Mendelson, Rachel Skolkin, Lee Kass, Rondi Frey, Lori Wilt, York Onnen (the President's Council on Physical Fitness and Sport); in Holland: Hank Fisher, Hans Iliohan, (The Dutch National Tourist Office); Marcel M. Claassen; in Switzerland: Enrico Zuffi, Tony Haeusler; in Ireland: Paddy Derivan, Roy Murray, Bill Maxwell, Kevin Shannon (The Irish Tourist Board); in New Zealand: Roy Harvey, Ron Richardson, John Guerin and Brian Leverell; in The UK: Bedford Pace (The British Tourist Office), Tony Rothwell, James Farrow; and in Germany: Gerd Pieper (The International Volkssport Association).

CONTENTS

PART THREE
Personalized Walking Programs

BASIC WALKING TECHNIQUES

LIST OF TABLES

How to Use This Book

WALKING WORKOUTS IS organized for serious exercise, progressing from basic training to high intensity workout routines. These workouts are for people at various degrees of physical fitness, not only recreational walkers, but also dancers, runners, hikers, weight lifters, and team sports players. The exercises described can be tailored to your age, body type, sex, athletic ability, or level of fitness. There are fast-paced routines for those who like to go fast, but there are also slow-paced routines that substitute resistance work for speed work.

We exercise to keep our bodies in good physical condition, to maintain muscle tone, and for strength, weight control, and relaxation. We hope in this way to look and feel better and to stay healthier. This package of physical maintenance is called "physical fitness." And physical fitness is the primary goal of regular exercise. Physical fitness includes ten elements: 1. strength, 2. speed, 3. endurance, 4. flexibility, 5. power, 6. agility, 7. coordination, 8. balance, 9. body control, and 10. well being. The Walking Workouts contribute to all ten elements. All four Workouts will build your strength, speed, endurance, flexibility, and power. And, the Walking Techniques specifically will improve your agility, coordination, balance, and body control. Daily walking either indoors or out, or both, will contribute to your feeling of well being.

If you follow the book in chapter order from beginning to end, you will discover how to make walking a serious and reliable routine for both aerobic and muscle training exercise. I recommend that you read it through from cover to cover before beginning to exercise in order to have the necessary information for each Workout program.

How This Book Is Organized

Part One: Getting Started

In this section I will explain how walking makes you physically fit and why you cannot afford *not* to walk. Then I will describe how to get ready for the Workouts (time, place, equipment).

Walking Techniques

Here I will show you the techniques you need to make ordinary walking a dynamic exercise. These techniques are necessary in order for the Workouts to work, so don't skip them. They include techniques on how to walk properly, how to stretch for flexibility, and how to use walking arm, leg, and body movements as muscle strengthening calisthenics.

Part Two: The Workouts

The four Walking Workouts in Part Three are self-contained. You can practice all of them as a weekly aerobic and body-building exercise, or you can alternate them on different exercise days.

The **Pacewalk Workout** is the basic aerobic walking routine. You should learn it before you do the other three.

The **Weightwalk Workout** combines weight training and walking. You will be using hand-held and ankle weights when doing these routines. You will also be building on what you have learned and practiced in *Pacewalking*.

The **Climbwalk Workout** is the highest intensity Walking Workout. It combines resistance and speed work to burn 1,000 calories an hour.

The **Dancewalk Workout** gives you a chance to combine most of the walking exercise techniques you have learned into one continuous medley of exercises.

Part Three: Personalized Walking Programs

In this section I will show you how to tailor the Workouts to your special needs and to your age, sex, fitness level, and athletic ability. In addition, I will discuss the joys of walking outdoors and show you how to use your indoor Walking Workouts out of doors. Chapter 5 in Part Four describes ways to use walking to help get rid of bad habits and to control your weight.

Some Hints

Proceed in Graduated Steps

Don't rush the training program, especially if you are just beginning to walk for exercise or are just starting to exercise routinely. Even if you are physically fit from some other kind of exercise, don't jump ahead, particularly on the weight training and stair climbing routines. If you do, you will probably be sore, and it will set your training program back a few days.

Practice the Walking Techniques

Even when you are not exercisewalking, the techniques should be practiced. Take the six-week start-up period seriously. It will give you time to get your walking muscles in shape. Remember, the Workouts require some skill development, and it's worth taking the time in the beginning to learn these skills properly.

Stick to the Basics

Don't become creative too soon by varying your Workout routine before you master it. You'll see that there is enough variety and complexity in the Walking Workouts to keep you busy and interested for at least four months. The key is to first make the Walking Workouts a habit, then to be creative.

Remember the Warm-ups and Cool-downs

Finally, do not neglect your warm-ups and cool-downs. Walking Workouts is a high intensity aerobic exercise, and if you don't allow warm-up exercises before and a gradual cooling down afterward, you can injure yourself.

Warning: When I say walking is "injury free" I mean that through continual practice of it you will not damage your joints, muscles, and ligaments as you can in exercises where you jump and bounce. That's because with walking you land with one fourth the pressure on your body parts that you do with running or jumping. Don't confuse this injury free action with injuries caused by falling accidents and overtraining. You have to take care not to overdo it during any vigorous workout, including a walking workout. You have to be careful when combining walking and weight training that you do not overload your body. You also have to take care when walking fast that you walk on smooth and safe surfaces. Take special care when walking stairs and inclines, where there is always danger of getting injured from falling, as there is with any sports and exercises.

Introduction

SINCE 1981, BOTH walking and exercise have taken a great leap forward. The number of organized walking events and clubs has grown by the hundreds, and walking has increasingly become the aerobic exercise substitute for jogging in America. Why? Because you can't use running as a regular lifetime exercise. The body was not built for running. Polls of regular runners show injury rates as high as 60 to 75 percent.

But what about those 80-year-old men and women who run the 26-mile marathons? With few exceptions, those eighty year olds started their running program only three to five years ago. Walkers, on the other hand, maintain a lifetime walking habit ranging from 20 to 80 years. In fact, for the last 250 years, dedicated 70- and 80-year-old walkers like Edward Payson Weston, John Muir, Oliver Wendell Holmes, Ray Bradbury, and Harry Truman, have been recording totals of lifetime walking miles as high as 200,000. Can you imagine what this number of miles would do to the back, ankle, and knee joints of a runner? Walking is a logical injury-free alternative to running.

However, a brisk walk, while good for your health, is not going to burn the 1,200 calories per week most experts prescribe as a minimum for basic fitness. If you want to manage your weight, muscle tone, and cardiovascular fitness, you have to have a reliable program that will produce results and encourage you to stick with it. *Walking Workouts* provides this program. It is the first exercise book to get serious about walking, taking it indoors, and using it in a way it has never been used before, as both an aerobic conditioner and a body-building regime. In a series of four progressive Walking Workouts, employing speedwork, resistance, weight training, and endurance training, I will show both beginners and advanced athletes how to turn walking into a vigorous workout and make the "walking body" the ultimate exercise machine.

Why Walking?

Injury-free Exercise

The walking body is like a weight training and aerobic exercise machine built into one. With one single synchronized movement you can more easily exercise all your body parts, including the lungs and heart, by walking than by any other activity. And you can do it without injury. Walking is the safest aerobic exercise, giving you all the cardiovascular training effects you get from running, jumping, and aerobic dancing, but none of the injuries. This is because exercises in which your body leaves the ground produce four times the stress on your muscular-skeletal system. Walking is biomechanically distinguishable from other activities like jumping, swimming, running, and bicycling in that one foot always stays on the ground. The pressure on the walking body is one-third to one-fourth that of other exercise activities. When you take a running step or jump into the air, you land with a force equal to four times your body weight. When you take a *walking* step, you land with a force equivalent to one time your body weight.

Walking straightforward with parallel leg and arm swinging is the most natural way you can use the ankle, knee, hip, elbow, and shoulder joints without putting the undue stress on them that occurs with exercises or sports movements that go from side to side (like tennis) or involve overextending the range of movement (like the snapping motion when throwing a ball). Not that these movements should be prohibited, but they should not be repeated constantly.

Also, injury-prone exercises like running require a lot of time for rest and recuperation. Often injury recuperation time wipes out the fitness benefits that come with repetition and requires you to start your exercise program over from the beginning.

Furthermore, many joggers and aerobic dancers are forced to permanently abandon their "off-the-ground" exercises because of knee or back injuries. At this point, walking may be their only exercise alternative. Runners, for example, who are able to continue running as an exercise for more than five years are either lucky or "built like runners." Only about 10 percent of the population have the body type for running, i.e., ectomorphic, where the ratio of body height to body weight is two pounds for every inch of height. That means a six-foot person should not weigh more than 144 pounds. The rest of us have a much greater ratio of weight to height, making any jumping or bouncing activity cause greater stress on our joints and back muscles.

Can a little bit of jogging, bouncing, or jumping mixed in with other exercise movements really be that harmful? Yes, if you do regular aerobic exercises that involve these three movements, you will feel the negative effects as joint and back pain.

Exercises for Everywhere

The Walking Workouts in this book can be done indoors or outdoors. You can do them while watching TV or listening to music. You don't have to plan a hiking trip or go out in below-freezing weather. All you have to do is get out of your easy chair and clear a space of about five feet by five feet. Once you've mastered the basic Workout routines, you can practice them indoors or on city streets, country roads, wilderness treks, long distance hikes, mountain hikes, and in shopping malls.

No Talent Required

The Walking Workouts I describe do require certain special walking techniques, but you do not need any special athletic ability to do them. They are suitable for everybody and they can be practiced every day. And, of course, you do not need special equipment. Your "walking body" is the ultimate exercise machine.

A Social Activity

Walking is fun in a group. You can practice your Walking Workouts with friends and family members at your health club, on vacation or in the local park.

Combines Well with Other Exercises

While the Walking Workouts program is a complete and self-contained exercise program, if you don't want to make walking your primary exercise, you don't have to. The Workouts combine well, as a primary or supplementary exercise, with bicycling, swimming, running, dancing, bodybuilding, skiing, racquet sports, and hiking.

If you are a runner, jogger, or bicyclist, the Walking Workouts program will help develop your leg and upper body muscles in a more balanced way. They will also help you burn calories and offer a relaxation exercise on your off days. For bicyclists, in particular, the weight-loaded Workouts will give sufficient muscle training and act as an aerobic alternative to bicycling.

If you are a dancer, alpine skier, body-builder, or racquet sports player, you can do Walking Workouts instead of jogging. The Workouts won't hurt or injure your knees and back. If you are a swimmer or cross country skier, Walking Workouts can serve as your off-season training regimen or step in as a workout when the facilities, time, or place are inconvenient.

Weight Loading with Less Stress

Because walking is not overly stressful to joints, ligaments, and muscles, it allows you to weight load different parts of your body and do more work rhythmically with less stress. A weight-loaded walker in excellent physical condition can carry from 40 to 100 percent of his body weight and still put only half the pressure on his joints and limbs as a runner without any weight load at all.

On the walking "machine" (your body) it is possible to add up to 100 percent of your body weight, do 200 arm and leg repetitions a minute, climb a 90-degree slope, and have 180-degree leg motion and 360-degree arm motion. Simultaneously you can work more body parts at a higher rate of caloric burn than with any other single exercise. A weight-loaded walker, using the Stairmaster exercise machine (see Appendix, p. 204), or climbing a 45-degree incline at 120 steps per minute can burn 1,000 calories an hour.

I should point out here that while the Walking Workouts include aspects of both Power Walking and Heavy Hands, they differ from both. Power Walking involves weight loading exclusively to achieve aerobic training effect, while the Workouts include speed work, walking in place, walking calisthenics, and stair climbing workouts to provide greater technical

What Walking Isn't— Some Myths Exposed

Walking Is Slow and Boring

People think of walking as a slow, easy, boring activity. Nothing could be further from the truth. We have a mental picture of people strolling in parks or shuffling along as they recover from operations. But, in fact, walking is an antidote to boredom because it offers a wide range of activities, both light and strenuous, each activity providing different exercise values. And, to further ensure against boredom, walking can be combined with other activities like sight-seeing and good conversation.

As for pace, walking speeds vary from a slow shuffle at one mph to sprint walking at 10 mph. An average walker in the street averages a mile in 20 minutes, a backpacker does a mile in about 30 minutes, and a brisk walker can cover a level mile in from 12 to 17 minutes. Walkers trained in racewalking can walk a 6-minute mile (which is pretty fast considering that the record for running a mile is still close to four minutes).

But Walking Workouts is not racewalking, a highly technical style of walking used in Olympic track and field competitions. Walking Workouts and racewalking differ from both a technical and an aesthetic point of view. Racewalkers were the pioneers in developing the different walking movements that make walking faster and more efficient. Their contribution to the Workouts can be seen in the Pacewalking Workouts in Chapter 1. But the Workouts, unlike racewalking, involve resistance and weight training, providing a higher degree of muscular development and strength. The Walking Workouts will train you to walk shorter

variety and sophistication. In other words, it is a more comprehensive exercise program than Power Walking. Heavy Hands includes other exercise movements that involve jumping or leaving the ground with weights attached to your arms. Walking Workouts is exclusively a walking exercise system and, while Heavy Hands has a walking component, it does not involve the full range and variety of walking movements found in the Walking Workouts program.

distances, for example, 220 to 880 yards at a 9-minute pace without racewalking. By walking in place, an exerciser can take as many as 200 steps per minute which, translated into road-minute-miles, amounts to a 7-minute-mile pace. Some walkers can go even faster in place because they have a natural leg speed of 300 steps per minute or the equivalent of a 5- to 6-minute mile.

Walking Doesn't Give You Enough Exercise

It is true that a moderate paced walk or even a brisk walk will not condition your skeletal muscles and cardiovascular system fully. But the basic walking movement has the potential to be the most comprehensive conditioning system. Walking as a workout trains all the body's muscles, burns calories, and improves circulation. It involves continuous rhythmic movements of all the major muscle groups.

Walking Does Not Provide Enough Aerobic Conditioning

Brisk walking and resistance walking do. You can develop the aerobic training effect with the four Workouts in this book. The Weightwalking and Climbwalking Workouts, especially, provide the most efficient aerobic conditioners, but even slow walking can give you some aerobic training benefits.

Walking Is for Old or Injured People

Walking *is* the exercise for the old and injured. It is also the recommended exercise for recuperating post-operative patients, for persons with high blood pressure, arthritis, and a myriad of other diseases. But walking is also increasingly the exercise of choice for athletes who have been injured in sports like running, aerobic dance, and skiing. Walking is the activity of choice for the majority of Americans. A recent recreational survey from the U.S. Bureau of the Census shows that 53 percent of all Americans above the age of twelve say walking is their favorite recreation. This means 93 million people claim walking is their favorite pastime.

It is time for a new exercise philosophy in America, one that makes aerobic exercise accessible to the majority, but eliminates high injury and dropout rates. *Walking Workouts* provides the answer. It is the best exercise prescription for all Americans. In truth, walking is the *only* safe and effective lifetime exercise.

Part One

GETTING

STARTED

How Walking Makes You Physically Fit

The Ultimate Exercise Machine

Your body is built for walking. When you habitually sit, stand, or lie down, your blood pools in your lower extremities and your muscles and bones begin to atrophy. But when you walk, your body becomes a dynamic exercise machine that uses almost all your bones and muscles. This "walking machine" has its own computer (the brain) for keeping track of the amount of exercise you do; it also monitors and regulates the intensity of your exercise by slowing down or speeding up the pace, as required.

Your walking machine has a number of built-in attachments (limbs) whose natural weights serve as exercise weight loads, and you can add extra weights to load your arms, waist, or legs, if desired.

In the *Walking Workouts* your body is the ultimate exercise machine. As you begin your Workouts program, think of

your body in these terms, for it truly is an exercise machine, capable of flexibility, strength, and endurance training, individually or in combination with other sports or exercises.

Basic Walking: The Whole Body

Walking is defined as the body moving continuously and rhythmically with one foot on the ground, while the other foot swings and comes down in the direction of travel. As one leg moves, the opposite arm swings in the direction of travel to act as a counterbalancing force. This continuous swinging of the limbs involves all the major muscle groups and uses the cardiovascular system to transport oxygen and nutrients to the working muscles. Because walking puts equal stress on the whole body (i.e., it does not favor one particular muscle group over another), it is considered one of the primary cardio-vascular conditioning exercises.

Although we take walking for granted, it is not simple. It is actually a complicated system of subsidiary and complementary body movements that is almost as complex as dance or gymnastics.

The Walking Cycle

The *walking cycle* is a basic walking action which includes three steps forward, measured from the heel contact of one foot to the heel contact of the other foot and then back to the heel contact of the starting foot. During this cycle of steps, there are *support phases* and a *swing phase;* one leg swings forward (the swing phase), while the other leg supports it (the single support phase). There is a brief period before the rear leg begins its forward swing, when both feet are on the ground supporting the body (the double support phase), as the weight shifts from the back leg to the forward leg. The forward foot is performing a *heel strike* and the back foot a *toe push-off.* The single and double support phases of walking are what distinguish it from running where both feet can be airborne simultaneously.

Swing Phase: The swing phase starts with the push-off by the ball of the rear foot. The iliacus contracts to initiate hip muscle flexion, the calf muscles (triceps surae) contract long enough to raise the heel, and the quadriceps bend the knee and lift the leg off the ground. The buttocks muscles are elongated as the leg swings forward. The further forward the hip is extended, the more the hip and buttocks muscles are used (gluteus maximus, medius, and minimus).

The shin muscles and toe extensor muscles raise the toes up, flexing the ankles so the heel can strike the ground.

The adductors (hip flexors) are activated at the beginning and end of the swing phase. The calf muscles (ankle flexors) and quadricep muscles (knee extensor) are used at the end of the swing phase.

When the heel strikes the ground, the quadriceps, shin, and hamstrings are fully extended. As the body moves forward past its center of gravity, the ankle begins to be flexed by the calf muscle, the knee is bent back by the hamstring muscles, and the middle body is moved forward by the hip flexor.

The deltoid or shoulder muscles become active as the arm swings back (anterior to middle to posterior) and are again active as the arm swings forward (posterior to middle to anterior).

Meanwhile, the bicep muscle (brachioradialis) keeps the arm bent, and the tricep muscle assists the shoulder muscles in swinging the arm backward. By keeping the hands slightly bent in an open fist while swinging, you also activate the muscles in the forearms.

Most of the leg and arm muscles are used during the swing phase to start up, stop, and change the direction of the swinging limbs.

The beginning and end of the leg stance phase are the periods when muscles are at maximum contraction. The buttocks muscle is at maximum contraction at the beginning of the phase.

The ankle extensor (calf muscle), knee extensor (quadriceps muscle), and the hip flexors are activated during the support phase.

The muscular activity of walking assists the heart in circulating blood throughout the body, and the act of breathing expands the chest and lungs.

CHAPTER

2 Learning How to Walk Again

I PROMISED THAT THE Walking Workouts would require no special sports skills, and they don't. They do, however, require that you learn certain walking techniques. These techniques will ensure that you are walking correctly so that you will get the most benefit from the dynamic Workouts.

In this chapter I will introduce the basic walking techniques you will need to begin the Starter Program and the Daily Walk routine. I will add techniques as they are needed to do each of the four Walking Workouts.

The Starter Program

This is a six-week session during which you will learn the basic walking skills and get into shape for the Workouts. If you are already in good physical condition, practice the techniques in this chapter and use the Advanced Program to exercise before going on to Part Two. *Walking Workouts* is divided into two groups: Beginners and Advanced. If you are just starting an exercise program or are in poor or only fair physical condition, call yourself a "beginner" and follow the exercise routines for beginners whenever they are indicated.

Even if you are in good physical shape, start with the beginner routines, particularly for technical practice. Once you have mastered those, call yourself "advanced" and follow the advanced routines.

Be sure to check with your doctor before beginning your Walking Workout program, especially if you are out of shape, a smoker, have a family history of heart disease, or are over age 35.

Daily Walking

The best way to get into shape is to walk daily. Even if you are in good shape, you will need Daily Walking to help you relax, control your weight, and maintain your fitness level.

As soon as you have learned the basic walking techniques, begin a daily walking-for-miles program. Strive to walk from two to four miles per day as part of your daily walking program. Begin by walking 15 minutes a day at a relaxed pace (2 to 3 mph) and gradually increase the time and distance over the six-week Starter Program period by adding 5 minutes to your daily walking time each week. At the end of the six-week period, your daily walking time should be up to 45 minutes, or your walking distance should be at least two miles and as many as three miles a day. If you have more time or are particularly energetic, add 10 minutes instead of 5, and try to reach four miles by the end of the six weeks. While it is preferable to do continuous walking if time permits, you can split up your Daily Walking into two or more walks of 10 to 15 minutes each.

After the second week, begin to monitor your walking speed and try to maintain at least a 3 mph or 20-minute-per-mile pace. If you are more energetic, try walking 3.5 mph. A word of caution, however:

TABLE 1: BEGINNER DAILY WALKING MILEAGE

	Miles per walk	Freq	Cumulative weekly mileage	Exercise calories
Level I Goal 2 miles without rest (not more than 5 minutes per hour). (Daily walking, 7 times a week)				
Week #1	⅛	×7	⅞	100
2	¼	×7	2	200
3	½	×7	3½	350
4	¾	×7	5¼	500
5	1	×7	7	700
6	2	×3+1	7	700
Final mileage goal	— 2		— 7	— 700
Level II Goal 4 miles without rest (3 times a week)				
Week #1	2	×3+1	7	700
2	2½	×3	7½	750
3	2¾	×3	8¼	800
4	3	×3	9	900
5	3½	×3	10½	1050
6	4	×3	12	1200
Final mileage goal	— 4		— 12	— 1200

during this Starter Program, it is important not to overdo the pace. Don't go faster than 3.5 mph or walk more than five miles per day because you may burn yourself out and be too tired for the next day's walking. Tables 1 (p. 15) and 2 (p. 16) show beginner and advanced walking schedules for the six-week Starter Program.

TABLE 2: ADVANCED DAILY WALKING MILEAGE

	Miles per walk	Freq	Cumulative weekly mileage	Exercise calories
Level III				
Week #1	4	×3	12	1200
2	4½	×3	13½	1350
3	5½	×3	15	1500
4	5½	×3	16½	1650
5	6	×3	18	1800
6	6	×3	18	1800
Final mileage goal	6		18	1800
Level IV				
Week #1	6	×3	18	1800
2	6½	×3	19½	1950
3	7	×3	21	2100
4	7½	×3	22½	2250
5	8	×3	24	2400
6	8	×3	24	2400
Final mileage goal	8		24	2400
Level V				
Week #1	8	×3	24	2400
2	8½	×3	25½	2550
3	9	×3	27	2700
4	9½	×3	28½	2850
5	10	×3	30	3000
6	10	×3	30	3000
Final mileage goal	10		30	3000

Walking Techniques

THE WALKING TECHNIQUES in this chapter will show you how to put more speed, muscular effort, and range of movement into your regular walking. In the process you will improve your balance, coordination, body control, and agility.

In order to make walking a vigorous workout, you also need to do stretching exercises. Therefore, a series of stretching exercises is included to further increase your muscle and joint flexibility. Later you will be able to turn both the walking tech-niques and the stretching exercises into muscle strengthening calisthenics. Even after you have started working out, you will probably want to turn back to this sec-tion of the book to continue refining your walking techniques and to apply various stretching exercises to the four Walking Workouts. *Don't skip this section.* It con-tains the key ingredients for making the Workouts work for you. Practice each walking technique separately before put-ting them together in a continuous walk-ing movement.

Holding Proper Posture

The Basic Starting Position

Stand with your feet parallel, hip-distance apart (3 to 5 inches), toes pointed in the direction of travel. Your head should be erect, shoulders pulled back but relaxed, back straight. Focus your eyes forward and look out approximately fifteen feet. (If you look any closer, you'll throw off your pos-ture.) Your hands should hang at your sides, palms turned inward, fingers stretched out and relaxed. Your knees should be slightly bent (not locked). Pull your stomach in, tuck in your buttocks.

Technique
#1

Check your posture in a mirror or have a partner look it over. This is the Basic Starting Position.

For the smoothest walking movements, your body must be properly aligned from head to foot. A crooked or bent posture will produce side-to-side swinging and extraneous motion leading to lost energy. Don't bend your body too far forward (not more than 5 degrees off center) when moving forward, or too far backward (not more than 10 degrees) when leaning back to walk down an incline; bending will slow you down by shifting your center of gravity. On flat ground, your body should always be in its normal upright position.

If you have problems holding the proper posture, practice the posture correction exercises below.

Posture Correction Exercises

Correcting Your Posture While Standing in Place Use this exercise to test and improve the posture of the upper torso.

Stand in the Basic Starting Position, your back against a wall, your feet parallel and about 2 to 4 inches from the wall. First, lean back against the wall, then bend over with your knees slightly bent and try to touch your toes. From this position, slowly straighten up your body so that every part of your back unrolls, touching the wall. It is important that the small of the back not arch away from the wall when the shoulders are pressed against it.

Correcting Your Posture While Walking After you have established an erect posture in the standing position, practice holding it while you walk. Control your head movement; don't look down at your feet, but straight out in front of you. Try walking while you balance a book on your head.

If you continue to have poor posture, practice exercises for strengthening your stomach muscles and lower back.

The Stride Stance Position

From the Basic Starting Position, take one step forward with your left foot and freeze in this position. This is the *Stride Stance* (the double support phase of the walking cycle). Certain walking techniques start from this position.

In the Stride Stance Position, your feet should remain parallel, toes pointed in the direction of travel. Correct your back foot now, the toes are probably pointed out. If it is hard for you to hold this position, assume a wider stance (your feet should be at least shoulder width apart). Keep your head erect, shoulders held back and relaxed, eyes forward. Buttocks and stomach muscles should be tucked and pulled in. Swing your right arm forward and your left arm back. Hold them in this position. Your arms should be slightly bent and your right arm should be parallel with the forward or left leg. Your left arm should be extended back and parallel to the rear leg as shown in the photo.

Resume the Basic Starting Position by stepping back with your left foot and bringing your feet parallel, your arms again hanging relaxed by your side, toes pointed in the direction of travel. It is difficult in the beginning to hold the Stride Stance Position too long; with practice it gets easier.

Technique #2

The Leg Swing/Pull Through

From the Basic Starting Position, swing your left foot forward 6 to 12 inches off the ground. Your toes should remain pointed in the direction of travel. Raise your heel first and push off with your toes.

Keep your rear leg straight, toes pointed in the direction of travel. As soon as your forward foot hits the ground, straighten it. You are once again in the Stride Stance Position.

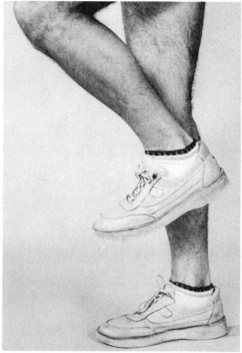

From this position, start your rear leg swing by pushing off with your toes. Use the thigh and shin muscles at the front of your leg to guide your leg as you pull it under your body, keeping your knee slightly bent, your toes pointed in the direction of travel. Begin to shift your arms so your forward arm (opposite your forward leg) swings back and your back arm swings forward. Once your leg is forward of your body, begin to straighten it. Don't straighten it completely until your foot makes contact with the ground.

Technique #3

The Heel Strike

You should land on the outer edge of your heel with your toes pointed upward at an angle of 40 degrees with the ground so that the forward moving foot makes contact with the ground at the heel, not at the mid-foot or the ball of the foot. Straighten your leg as soon as your heel makes contact with the ground.

If you hear a flopping sound when you walk, it is probably because you are not landing on your heel, but on the flat part of your foot.

Heel Walk Exercise

Practice walking on your heels (10 steps with each foot), so you can feel what it means to land on your heel.

Technique #4

Proper Foot Placement

Your feet should be placed 3 to 5 inches apart for regular walking, closer together (1 to 3 inches apart) for faster walking. Don't let your legs brush at the thighs or knees as they pass each other. Widen your foot placement for walking with weight loads or on rough terrain.

If your feet are not parallel, you will be poorly balanced. Practice walking next to a marked straight line, taking care to place your feet alongside it in a parallel and equidistant fashion.

Technique #5

The Heel-Toe Roll

After your heel strikes the ground, begin to roll the forward foot on its outer edge until you reach the toes. Your foot should be turned outward enough so you can fit your fingers under the inside of your foot.

The outer edge of your foot is the smoothest or roundest edge for a forward smooth rolling motion. It acts as a natural rocker bottom for continuous forward motion. As you roll your foot forward on the outer edge, turn it slightly outward. This will keep your knee from turning in or pronating.

Heel-Toe Roll Exercise

Practice the heel-toe roll with both feet together, rolling from your heel up to your toes and back again.

Technique #6

The Toe-Off

From the Stride Stance position, push off with the ball of your foot, but do not break contact with the ground until you have completely rolled up onto your toes. In walking there is more rolling and pulling motion than the kicking-off motion used in running. That's why this is called the toe-off, and not the kick-off.

If you do not point your toes in the direction of travel as you push off, your body will go to one side. This produces excessive side-to-side swaying and will put undue stress on your joints.

Toe-Off Exercise

Practice the toe-off ten times by raising yourself onto your toes with both feet at the same time. This will enable you to execute a more powerful toe-off for faster walking.

Caution: If your foot leaves the ground too soon, that is, before it has rolled off the ball of your foot onto your toes, you can lose as much as three inches on each step. One of your goals in turning walking into a workout is to walk faster. A longer stride will help you do this, so you want to be very careful not to lose any inches on your step. If your body rises and falls each time you step, you are pushing off from the ball of your foot, not from your toes. Reduce your walking speed and concentrate on the toe-off. Also practice stretching exercises for better hip and ankle mobility (see p. 34).

Synchronized Arm Swings with Breathing

Technique #7

From the Basic Starting Position, practice swinging your arms back and forth. Hold each hand in an open fist, palms extended inward, fingers curled but loose and relaxed. Swing your arms back and forth in a natural arc. On the forward swing your arm should be at least as high as your shoulders. On the back swing let your hand go back as far as your flexibility will allow.

Breathe rhythmically as you swing your arms. Practice 20 arm swings, 10 with each arm. Breathe in on the right swing, out on the left.

PROPER BREATHING

Synchronized, deep breathing is important to good Workouts because it brings maximum oxygen to your working muscles. Use your breathing to regulate your Workout speed.

Diaphragm Breathing

Practice breathing using your diaphragm rather than your chest. To breathe deeply you must become more conscious of the act of breathing. During normal walking, practice breathing by imitating the breathing you do while sleeping or smelling. This will help you breathe correctly.

Diaphragm Breathing Exercise

1. Stand with your feet shoulder-width apart, toes pointed in the direction of travel, wrists crossed in front of you.

2. Slowly raise your arms forward and up over your head in an arc, while inhaling air through your nostrils, using your diaphragm. (Your stomach should expand as you inhale.)

3. Once your arms are over your head, inhale again until your diaphragm is filled; then let your chest expand to fill your lungs to full capacity.

4. Lower your arms slowly to your side, exhaling air from your mouth. Force the air out by pressing your arms with palms down until the lungs are completely empty.

5. Return to original position with your wrists crossed at your waist and repeat the exercise four more times.

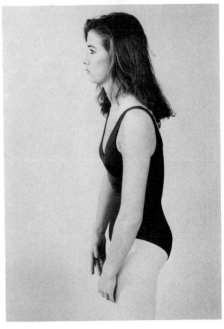

Belly Breathing Exercise Practice belly breathing by bending over and placing your hands on your knees. Take a deep breath through your nose or mouth while pushing your stomach out. Then exhale forcefully through your mouth using your stomach and rib cage. Try to get every last bit of breath out. Suck in your stomach and hold this position without breathing for 5 to 10 seconds.

Use belly breathing whenever you can during the exercises and Workouts that follow.

Remember: When doing the Walking Workouts, it is important to breathe rhythmically by synchronizing your breathing with your movements. *Inhale when you stress your muscles or work against gravity (lifting up, for example); exhale when you relax.*

**Technique
#8**

IN PLACE WALKING STEPS

There are certain special steps you need to know to practice your walking techniques in place (a 5′ × 5′ area). These are not really techniques, but a series of arm and leg movements. When walking in place, modify your heel strike by using a *forefoot strike*. Instead of making contact with your heel first, strike with your forefoot (the ball of your foot) first. Roll back to your heel and then forward to your toes again before pushing off or up (in the case of climbing up or down).

When side stepping or doing cross-over steps, land on the outer edge of your foot and roll to the inside edge.

Here are some specifics that make walking a multidirectional, multidimensional workout exercise.

Walking In Place Leg Lifts

When you walk in place you use the same basic 3-step walking cycle that you use in regular walking, but the intervals are shorter because instead of stepping out, you step up. While one leg is lifting up, the other supports the body (single support phase). When you bring the leg back down and shift your weight to the other side, both feet are briefly on the ground at the same time (double support phase).

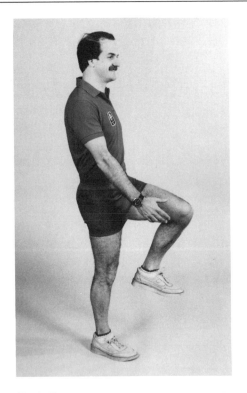

Back Steps

Walking backwards works and stretches the back of the leg muscles. Of all the walking steps, this one is the most difficult to master because you have to keep looking over your shoulder to stay on track.

Unlike forward steps, back steps start with the toes and roll back to the heel. As a result, you lift and pull the leg under your body more than pushing it off. The push-off (now called a pull-back) comes at the heel, causing the leg to bend back further so that the hamstrings (back of thigh) get more of a stretch, and the quadriceps (front of thigh) and shin muscles are used more. Back stepping is used during walking in place exercises and stair work.

Leg Crossover Steps

Walk sideways by crossing one leg over the other; three steps to the left and three steps back to the right. Place the moving leg 4 to 12 inches from the supporting leg. The farther you stretch the crossover step, the more you will work the adductors (inner thigh muscles). Crossover steps are used in the Weightwalk and Climb Workouts. When crossing over you make contact with the outer edge of your foot first, rolling to the instep.

Side Steps

Keeping your feet parallel, step to the side and bring the lagging foot up to the one stepping first. You can take three steps to the left and three steps back to the right without having to leave your 5' × 5' workout space.

Synchronized Arm and Leg Swings

From the Basic Starting Position practice swinging your arms and legs in a parallel, rhythmic fashion, synchronized with breathing cadences. Make sure your hands are relaxed, fists loosely clenched. This will keep you from tensing your arms and shoulders during the swing motion. Walk in place, taking three steps forward, lifting the foot opposite the swinging arm. Synchronize your movements with your breathing. Your arms should swing naturally as you walk, acting as a counterbalance to your swinging legs. Your arms can be bent or straight when swinging. If you bend them, you can move both your arms and legs faster because your arms have a shorter distance to travel.

Practice synchronized arm and leg swings while looking in the mirror to observe whether you are maintaining proper posture. If you try walking fast without swinging your arms, you will see the important role your arms play in maintaining forward momentum.

Putting It All Together

Practice your walking techniques, particularly arm swinging and synchronized breathing, while doing a medley of front, back, and side-to-side steps. Use the following breathing cadences to help you keep the rhythm.

4-Count Cadence Practice a 4-count cadence by inhaling on the first two steps, exhaling on the next two.

2-Count Cadence Practice a 2-count cadence by inhaling on one step, exhaling on the next.

The Warm-Up Walk

The warm-up walk is designed to get your blood circulating and your muscles warm and limber. Start each Walking Workout with a brisk warm-up walk of 2 to 5 minutes. You can count your daily morning walk, if you do one, as your warm-up walk. At the end of the warm-up walk you should be sweating slightly, but not out of breath.

Before each Walking Workout you will be doing two warm-up walks; one to warm up your muscles before stretching, the other to start your heart rate rising before aerobics.

You can do your warm-up walk in place or on the move.

Warm-Up Walking on the Move

When warm-up walking outside, take long strides and swing your arms briskly to shoulder height. Walk at the rate of 3 to 4 mph or about 90 to 120 spm (steps per minute) (see Table 3: Walking Speed, p. 33). As you become more fit, move your arms and legs faster so that you begin to

TABLE 3: WALKING SPEED CONVERSIONS
Use this chart to convert walking on the move (mph or minute miles, mm) into walking in place (step and arm repetitions)

Miles per Hour (MPH)	Minute Miles (MM)	Steps (Arms Repetition) per Minute (SPM)
1.00	60	30
1.25	48	35
1.50	40	40
1.75	34.3	43
2.00	30	45
2.25	26.7	55
2.50	24	60
2.75	21.8	75
3.00	20	90
3.25	18.5	95
3.50	17	100
3.75	16	110
4.00	15	120
4.25	14	125
4.50	13	130
4.75	12.6	135
5.00	12	140
5.25	11	145
5.50	10.9	150
5.75	10.4	155
6.00	10	160
6.25	9.6	163
6.50	9.2	165
6.75	8.9	168
7.00	8.6	170
7.25	8.3	173
7.50	8.	175
7.75	7.7	178
8.00	7.5	180
8.25	7.3	183
8.50	7.	185
8.75	6.9	188
9.00	6.7	190
9.25	6.5	193
9.50	6.3	195
9.75	6.2	198
10.00	6.	200

sweat within 2 to 5 minutes. Vary your warm-up routine by doing a series of different arm swings such as windmills, crossover pumps, and cradle swings (see p. 42).

Warm-Up Walking In Place

Do your warm-up walk in place by lifting each leg at least 12 inches off the ground while simultaneously swinging your opposite arm, keeping it slightly bent and at shoulder height. As your strength and stamina improve, increase the height of your leg lifts and the length of your arm arcs. Diversify your warm-up walk by doing a variety of arm swings, accompanied by 3-step front-and-back marching, crossover, and side steps (see p. 31).

Stretching

Stretching improves the range of limb and body motion. It helps you become more flexible and makes your walking exercises more dynamic by reducing the strain on muscles that are being vigorously worked. Many stretching exercises are also strengthening exercises.

Stretching improves walking in five specific areas.

1. Stretching gives better ankle joint flexibility for the heel-toe roll and the toe-off.

2. It increases the range of hip movement. This, in turn, increases stride length and leg speed.

3. Stretching the spine improves posture.

4. Stretching shoulder joints makes

them more flexible for faster and smoother arm action.

5. Stretching reduces soreness and the potential for muscle strain during weight training and walking.

Basic Stretches

There are four basic stretches, the Calf and Achilles Tendon Stretch, the Quadricep and Ankle Stretch, the Hamstring Stretch, and the Flying Lunge Stretch. These should be done *before and after* each of the four Walking Workouts. Other stretches, specific to each Workout, will be added to these basic stretches.

Always Remember:
1. Breathe slowly and rhythmically while stretching, exhaling as you bend forward, inhaling as you go back. Don't hold your breath, and don't stretch to a point where you can't breathe.

2. Don't bounce while stretching. Bouncing tightens your muscles and allows them to resist the stretch. Instead, stretch and hold the position.

3. Don't overstretch. Concentrate on the area being stretched and, if the strain becomes too great (painful) on the muscle, return to a more comfortable position.

4. Don't wait for a stretching period to do a stretch. Any time a muscle, joint, or body area feels tight, take a few seconds to stretch it. Practice your stretching during non-Workout times, while waiting in line, for example, or watching TV.

5. Do a 2 to 5 minute warm-up walk *before any stretching*.

6. Make stretching a regular and relaxing habit.

The Basic Four Stretches

The Calf and Achilles Tendon Stretch This exercise stretches the lower back of your leg and will strengthen and improve the flexibility of your toe-off.

Stand, bracing yourself against a tree or wall, with your arms extended slightly over your head. Extend one leg forward with your knee bent. Press the heel of your back leg down against the ground and lean forward, keeping the leg straightened. Feel the stretch in your calf and Achilles tendon (above your heel). Hold this stretch for 15 to 20 counts.* Reverse the position of your legs to stretch the other calf.

*Note: Whenever a range of counts is given, beginners should practice at the low end of the range, advanced exercisers at the upper end of the range. Unless otherwise indicated, each count is one second in duration.

The Quadriceps and Ankle Stretch
Standing on your left foot (lean against a pole or wall to help you keep your balance), hold your right foot behind you with your right hand. Slowly pull your right heel toward the back of your leg, holding this position for 5 to 10 counts. As you develop better balance you will be able to do this stretch without holding on.

The Hamstring Stretch This stretching exercise will lengthen your walking stride. Raise your leg and prop the back of your heel on a sturdy surface such as a chair, fence, or the back of a park bench. Your heel should be raised between two and three feet off the ground. Straighten your raised leg while keeping your back leg slightly bent at the knee. Bend over at the waist, leaning with your arms stretched out toward your toes. If you can't reach your toes, grab hold of your ankle or fore-foot. Pull yourself slowly toward your toes and hold this position for 10 to 20 counts. Alternate your legs to stretch the other hamstring in the same way. If you point the toes of the supporting leg in the direction of the stretch, you will stretch your calf muscle as well.

The Beginner's Flying Lunge This is an easier version of the Flying Lunge, designed to stretch the calf and Achilles tendon. Step forward, front leg straightened, back foot in the toe-off position. As you bend your front knee, press your back heel down and hold for 8 to 15 counts. Repeat this stretch for each leg.

The Flying Lunge Stretch Take a giant step forward and bend your knee after you land on your heel. Keep your upper body erect, arms held out at your sides for balance. Your stance should be wide enough so you can keep your front and back toes pointed in the direction of travel. Slowly sink with your hips and touch the knee of your back leg to the ground. Hold this position for 6 to 8 counts. Switch legs and repeat the stretch.

The Flying Lunge stretches the upper body and the groin. To stretch your lower back, abdominal muscles, and chest, raise your arms up from the Flying Lunge position and arch backward.

In addition to the four basic stretches, there are a number of other stretching exercises you can do while walking to improve your flexibility and strength.

Neck Stretches

Head Bends

1. Stand in place with your feet parallel, shoulder width apart, toes pointed forward. Bend your head slowly in a smooth circular clockwise motion over the top of the shoulders, taking care not to bend it too far backward. Repeat slowly five times clockwise, then five times counterclockwise. If a particular area feels tight, stay with it until it loosens up.

2. Bend head straight forward, touching chin to chest, then straight back, then side to side. Hold each position for two counts and repeat exercise three times.

Arm and Shoulder Stretches

Shoulder Shrugs Raise up your shoulders as high as you can, hold for two counts and relax.

The Windmill Rotate shoulders by extending arms straight out to the side at shoulder level, then swinging arms forward and up over the head in a circular motion. Swing for 10 counts, then hold and stretch back to overhead position.

Single Arm Windmill Rotate each arm alternately (left, right, left, right) in a clockwise direction as the corresponding opposite leg lifts or steps. Repeat with each arm and in each direction for 6 to 12 counts. The accompanying photo shows how the upward swinging leg corresponds with the upward swinging arm for the clockwise rotations.

Triceps and Shoulder Stretch With your arms over your head, use one hand to slowly pull the elbow of your opposite arm behind your head. Hold for 15 counts on each arm.

Chest and Shoulder Stretch Interlock your fingers, palms facing toward you, and stretch your arms out in front of you. Now, turn your palms outward, keeping your fingers interlocked, and hold this position for 10 to 15 counts. Extend your arms overhead and hold for another 10 to 15 counts. Finally, stretch your arms out behind you, clasp your hands and rest them on something or grab onto a fence or doorway. Keep your chin and chest out, back straight and head erect. Hold for 10 to 15 counts.

Hips, Back, and Abdominal Stretches

Side and Spine Stretches Stand with your feet shoulder–width apart. Raise one arm, keeping the other by your side. Bend sideways, toward the lower arm, reaching with the raised arm over your ear. Keep your arms straight, hips square to the front. Slide your lower hand toward your knee as you bend. Hold for 10 to 20 counts. Repeat side bend to the other side and hold for 10 to 20 counts.

Twists With your feet shoulder–width apart and arms extended out to the sides, twist your head, arms, and upper body as far back as they will go while keeping your hips square to the front. Twist 2 to 5 counts to each side.

Back and Spine Reach Throughs With arms stretched forward, bend at the waist and at the knees and swing your arms through your legs. Return to the bent waist position. Repeat 5 to 10 counts.

Advanced: Start your reach throughs from a straight standing position. Bend down, reach through your legs and return upright. Now, bend your knees forward as you bend your back, arms, and shoulders backward. Hold for 5 counts.

Upper Back Stretch With both arms stretched in front of you, grab onto a bar or firm edge which is chest high or higher. Slowly drop your upper body down as you bend your knees slightly. Keep your heels flat on the ground. Do not bounce. Hold this position for 20 to 30 counts.

Lower Back Stretch—The Squat Stretch
This stretch is done from a standing position by slowly squatting with feet flat and toes pointed outward. Knees should be over big toes and feet should be 5 to 12 inches apart. If you have trouble with balance, try this stretch facing down a slope, leaning against a wall, or holding onto a chair or bar with your hands. Keep your head erect and use your thigh muscles, not your lower back, to raise and lower yourself. Hold the squat stretch position for as long as you can.

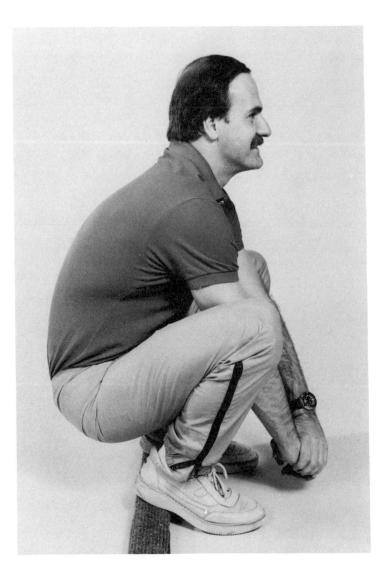

Hip Stretches

Hip exercises are the most important stretches you can do for the Walking Workouts. Increased hip flexibility allows you a longer stride and a more fluid walking motion. The following stretches will help increase your stride length.

Standing Back and Hip Stretch Stand with your feet parallel, shoulder-width apart. With your knees slightly bent, arms stretched down, bend slowly forward until you feel a slight stretch in your hamstring muscles. Stay in this position for about 20 counts. This movement will stretch your lower back, hips, groin and hamstring muscles.

Knee Ups Balance against a wall with one hand. While keeping your upper body erect, pull the opposite knee as close to your chest as you can. Keep your back straight and hold this position for 15 to 20 counts. This will gently stretch your hamstring and buttocks muscles as well as your hips. It is a good stretch for helping you to develop flexibility and balance for the marching exercises and the Weightwalk Workout.

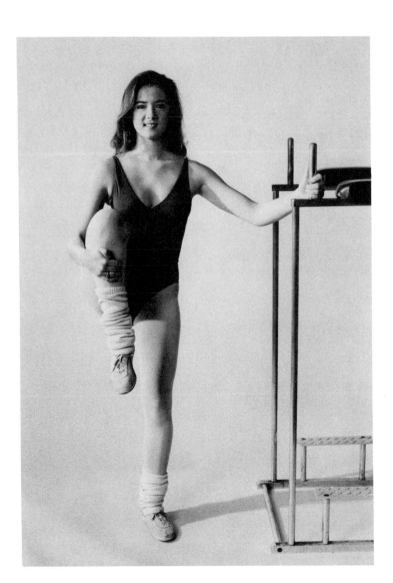

Standing Hip Stretch (Version 1) Stand with your feet shoulder–width apart, hands on hips. Bend to each side, straight over your hip as far as possible. Hold 15 to 20 counts on each side.

(Version 2) Stand with your feet shoulder–width apart. Place both hands just above your left knee and push your right hip forward. Rotate your pelvis forward and sideways for the stretch. Hold for 15 to 20 counts. Rest, and repeat on the other side.

Raised Leg Hip Stretch Put your foot on a waist-high surface. Start with your leg bent at the knee. Straighten it while pressing your hip and supporting leg forward. You should feel the stretch on the front hip of the supporting leg. Hold for 8 to 12 counts and repeat with the opposite leg forward. This position is similar to the basic Hamstring Stretch, but you do not bend your body as far forward and you do not let your hips relax.

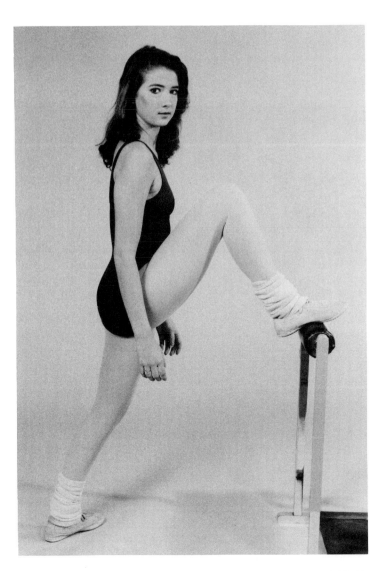

Lunges

These are the walker's all-purpose stretches. They stretch many of the muscles around the hip area.

Easy Lunge This is another version of the Flying Lunge, designed to stretch the hip, groin, and buttocks muscles. Bend your left foot forward until the knee is directly over the ankle. Hold for 15 to 30 counts.

Cool-Down Stretches

After every vigorous walk or Walking Workout session, take an extra five minutes to slow down your walking pace and do a series of selective stretching exercises. Start with the four basic stretches and then choose specific stretches for those areas of your body that you worked most during your session. Don't skip your cooldown stretches after a Workout.

Hang Over With your feet shoulder width apart, toes pointed in the direction of travel, slowly bend forward from the hips so that you do not overstress your lower back. Keep your knees slightly bent during this stretch and let your arms and neck hang, loose and relaxed. Bend until you feel a slight stretch in the back of your legs. It's not important if you can't touch your toes. Hold the stretch for 15 to 20 counts.

Inverted V This is a moderate stretch that works the whole body, including upper arms, shoulders, hamstrings, calves, Achilles tendons, and spine.

Start on your hands and knees. Be sure your hands are placed directly under your shoulders with your knees, heels, and toes together. Raise your hips as you push your heels and armpits in the direction of the floor. Your body should form an inverted V with your buttocks extended toward the ceiling. Breathe normally and hold this position for 10 to 20 counts.

Cross-Legged Stretch From a lying position, sit up with your legs crossed and lean forward. Hold and relax.

Bowlegged Stretch Lie on your back with the soles of your feet together and your knees bent. Relax and let gravity pull your knees down as you stretch your groin and relax your back. Gently rock your knees up and down to stretch the hip.

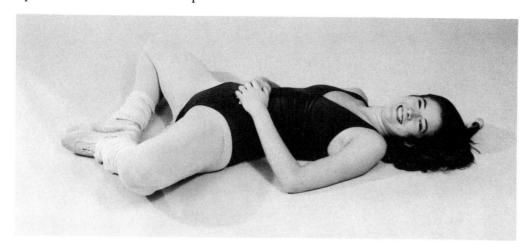

Hip and Back Relaxer Lie on your back, supporting yourself with your hands. Cross your legs and rock back and forth from the hip. (If you are more comfortable with your shoulders raised off the ground, that is okay, too.)

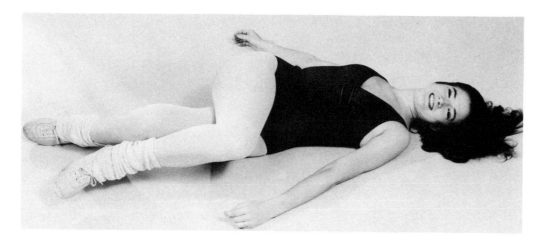

Groin and Lower Back Stretch In a seated position, put the soles of your feet together and clasp with both hands. Lean forward slowly, stretching the groin and lower back area. Hold 10 to 15 counts.

Spinal Twist Sitting with your right leg straight or tucked under as in the photo, cross your left leg over your knee. Rest your bent left elbow on the outside of your right knee. Use your elbow to keep your leg from moving during the stretch. Rest your left hand behind you and slowly turn your upper body and head, looking over your left shoulder. Keep your hips stationary by preventing your right leg from rotating. Breathe normally and hold position for 10 to 15 counts. Repeat stretch to the other side. The spinal twist stretches your upper and lower back as well as your hips and rib cage.

Overhead Leg Stretch From a lying position, slowly bring your legs over your head and roll backward, using your hands to support your hips. Breathe naturally and rhythmically and position your body in such a way that you can relax. Count to a minimum of 10.

Lying Down Neck Stretch While lying on your back with your knees bent, your feet flat on the floor, and your fingers clasped behind your head, pull your head slowly forward, stretching the back of the neck. Hold for 10 to 15 counts before dropping your head down again. Repeat 3 to 5 times.

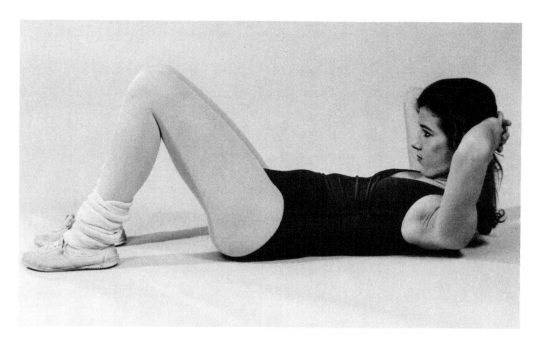

Elevating Your Feet While lying on the ground, rest your feet against a wall or other upright object. Your back should be flat and relaxed and your buttocks should not be closer than 5 inches to the wall. Simply relax in this position for at least 30 counts. Elevating your feet in between or after a long workout will help revitalize your legs.

Part Two

THE FOUR

WORKOUTS

Introduction: Organizing Your Workouts

The Importance of Having a Routine

Developing good habits takes effort, but once a habit is formed, it comes naturally. You have to work at developing a Workout routine in the beginning so that it becomes a natural part of your day. It's important to set aside a *specific* time and place when you first start. Once you have made walking a routine, you can practice it almost any time and any place. It usually takes a few months of regular practice to make the Workouts a habit. After that you can experiment with "exercising on the run," modifying your Workouts to suit various times and places or creating your own exercise routines.

Time

The best time to exercise is during natural breaks in the day: in the morning, at lunch, or before or after dinner. Being an early bird, I prefer to exercise in the morning, before the work day begins. Lunchtime Workouts are popular among exercisers who are also dieting and want to use part or all of their lunch period exercising instead of eating. Evening Workouts help you unwind and clear away the tensions and problems of the day. Set aside a minimum of three Walking Workout hours a week.

Place

When choosing a Workout place, it is important to find a relatively quiet spot, free from distractions. Try to avoid interruptions while you are learning your Workouts; you will need to concentrate in order to do them successfully. Once you master a Workout, you can take it "on the road," adding conversation or any number of distractions to your routine.

The Workouts can be done either indoors or outside, but you should have a clear area of at least five feet by five feet. If you are indoors, a full-length mirror, although not necessary, is desirable, because it will help you monitor the improvement in your techniques.

Since you will be swinging your arms and legs freely, determine if you have a clear space by making the widest range of walking movements. Measure out your Workout area by walking three steps forward and clearing overhead space at the same time by making windmill rotations with your arms. Then, extend your arms to the side as you do three steps to the left, back to center, and three steps to the right.

Music

Doing the Workouts to music helps you keep the beat. Your favorite album or tape is best. It should have a lively, steady beat, preferably with slow selections for the warm-up and cool-down and moderate to fast music for the calisthenic and aerobic conditioning portions. It's fun to be your own musical director. You can use a full symphony or arrange a selection from a variety of musical genres. For example:

Warm-up and Stretching: slow waltzes, ballads, love songs, Country Western, classical music (adagio movements).

Calisthenics and Aerobics: disco, rock 'n roll, march music, jazz, classical music (allegro movements).

Cool-down: same music as warm-up and stretching.

Practicing the Workouts

I have designed the four Walking Workouts to be practiced three to four times a week in a 30- to 60-minute exercise session. On each of the "off-days" it's good to do two to four miles of regular walking to relax and stay active for weight control.

Practice any of the four Workouts for six weeks at the beginner or advanced level, depending on your level of fitness and technical skill. If you are out of shape, it will take from twelve to sixteen weeks to get back into good condition. Increase the duration, speed, and intensity of the Workouts according to the various progressive conditioning tables throughout the book. I recommend following a systematic program to get in shape with the Walking Workouts.

Learn the Pacewalk Workout first and practice it the first six weeks to increase your walking speed and improve your cardiovascular conditioning and basic muscle strength. Next, do the Weightwalk Workout for six weeks to master the weight training skills, develop muscle strength, and further increase your aerobic conditioning. During the third six-week period, practice the Climb Workout. You should be in good physical shape by now and you should know most of the walking techniques. So, in the last six-week period, put all your techniques and exercise stamina together in the Dancewalk Workout, which combines the exercises from the previous three Walking Workouts and adds a few dancelike steps and arm movements.

I know some of you will be impatient to try all the Workouts right away, so I organized each as a self-contained unit. It's best, however, to learn and practice the Workouts separately, each for six weeks. Once you have mastered them, you can alternate them for variety and in order to train all your body parts.

Anatomy of a Walking Workout

Each of the four Workouts is divided into five segments. The minutes shown in parentheses indicate the time you should spend on that particular segment. Beginners should practice at the low end of the range; advanced walkers at the high end of the range.

Warm-Up Walk (2 to 5 minutes) This medium- to brisk-paced walk gets your blood circulating. You will be using the walk part of the Workout; that is, the pacewalk for the Pacewalk Workout, the weightwalk for the Weightwalk Workout, etc.

Stretching (5 to 10 minutes) Start with the four basic walker's stretches. If you have more time, complete the recommended series of stretches tailored for each Workout.

Techniques and Calisthenics (5 to 10 minutes) Each of the four Workouts introduces an increasingly more advanced set of walking techniques or special steps and arm movements you will need for the routine that follows.

You have now learned the basic walking techniques and stretching exercises you will need for the four Walking Workouts. Additional walking steps and techniques will be needed as you progress toward your goal of turning walking into a vigorous aerobic Workout. I will introduce these special steps and techniques as they are required.

Don't worry if the walking workouts seem too technical at first. With practice they will become second nature. After you learn good walking techniques, you will enjoy your walking and walking workouts without having to think much about technique. Once you have mastered a new technique, practice it as a calisthenic exercise during this 5 to 10 minute portion of your Workout by repeating the movement

a minimum of 8 times if you are a beginner and up to 20 times if you are advanced. As your physical conditioning progresses, repeat the techniques as calisthenic exercises in sets of two, three, and four, with 8 to 20 repetitions per set, or use hand-held or ankle weights for greater training effect. (See Weightwalk Calisthenics Table 16.)

Aerobic Walking Routines (15 to 30 minutes) This is the aerobic training portion of the Workout. You will use one of the three aerobic walking styles—fast walking (the Pacewalk), weight loaded walking (the Weightwalk) and/or hill walking and stair climbing (the Climbwalk Workout). These aerobic walking routines can be done over ground (on the move) or in place. The Dancewalk is a dancelike routine using walking. It combines Pace, Weight, and Climbwalking routines for the aerobic training portion, and moves you through the warm-up and stretching routines at a pace that can be synchronized to music.

Cool-Down Exercises (2 to 5 minutes) These are walking exercises which slowly reduce the aerobic walking pace and bring your pulse rate back down to just above resting. The cool-down exercises also include a select group of stretching exercises similar to, but not lasting as long as, the warm-up stretches.

Matching Your Workout to Your Fitness Level

I have devised a system of five Workout levels. Level I is for those who are in poor shape; the Workout is easy and designed to progress in small steps. If you are over 35 and have not done any exercise for the past year or more, start at Level I. If that

TABLE 4: FITNESS/WORKOUT LEVEL

Fitness Level	Workout Intensity
I = Poor	Easy
II = Fair	Slightly harder
III = Good	Intermediate/Advanced
IV = Very good	Advanced/High
V = Excellent	Highest

is too easy for you, go on to Level II which is for those who are in fair shape. Level III is for those in good physical condition, and Level IV is for those in *very* good condition. Level V is for those in excellent physical condition.

The Fitness/Workout Level System is a nice, neat little package to match your fitness level with the intensity level of your Workouts.

Follow the beginner versions of each Workout until you can progress to the next level. You will have to do a little experimenting. The Workout level should provide a challenge, but it should not make you sore the next day. On the other hand, if you choose too easy a level no improvement in your muscular strength and cardiovascular conditioning will take place. You will be burning calories, but you will not really be working out.

Strive to reach and maintain your Workout level at Level III. To go beyond that you must give an investment in time and energy that is really not necessary for everyday living. It's better to put that extra time and energy into more regular walking daily to relax, socialize, see the world, and burn extra calories.

If you want to work harder to feel better, be slimmer or train for competitive sports, Workout Levels IV and V are for you.

You do not need access to a special facility to test your fitness. The Walking Workout charts and tables can help you measure your fitness level and match it with the Workout level you should be doing.

Remember, you are probably not fit at the same level for all physical fitness components. For example, your aerobic fitness may be at Level III while your arm muscle fitness (strength) may only be at Level II. One of your exercise goals should be to reach the same high level in all areas. Make adjustments in your exercise program. If you're not very flexible, do a greater number of the stretching exercises. If your upper body is weak, do an additional set of the Weightwalk calisthenics.

Measuring and Charting Your Progress

Heart Training Rate To be aerobically efficient while you exercise, you should maintain your heartbeat in a "training zone" which is approximately 70 to 85% of your maximum heart rate. Your maximum heart rate is computed by subtracting your age from 220. (See Table 5.)

Step Rate Use the six-second-counting method to see how many leg and arm repetitions you can do in a minute which will, in turn, measure your walking speed and

PULSE COUNT

Use the six-second-pulse-counting method described below to determine if you are walking with your heartbeat in the training zone. (See Table 5: Your Aerobic Heart Training Rate, p. 71)

Counting Your Pulse: Six-Second Method
The easiest way to count your pulse is to lightly press the fingertips of your right hand on the radial artery of your left wrist. It runs along the inside of your wrist on the thumb side. Count the number of pulse beats in six seconds, counting the first beat 0, the next beat 1, etc. Multiply by 10 and you have the number of beats per minute (10 × 6 equals 60 seconds), without having to count beats for the whole 60 seconds.

Practice monitoring your pulse both at rest and while walking in place. Do it a few times until it feels comfortable. Stop reading and try it now.

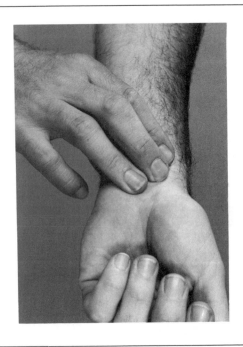

Workout pace. The Walking Speed Chart 3 translates step rate into miles per hour and minute miles for walking on the move. It also translates into a cadence count (Table 9, p. 90) to help you keep track of the intensity of your Workouts.

Maximum Speed, Maximum Weight Formulas You can estimate your training speed level and weight load level by taking 60 to 75% of your maximum speed while walking 100 yards and while carrying the maximum weight you can. The limit for weight, however, should not exceed 40% of your own body weight. Note that this level is below the training rate range (70 to 85% at which you work your cardiovascular system during aerobic exercise) but it is based on the same principle of working below your maximum capacity to exercise for training effect.

METS Using METS (derived from the word "metabolism") is the best way to measure the intensity of your exercise. METS measure your exercise intensity as a multiple of your resting rate of metabolism; that is, how many calories you burn over your resting metabolic rate. Your resting metabolic rate is 1 MET. Walking at 3 mph is 4 METS, walking with one-pound hand-held weights is 5 METS, stair climbing at 90 steps-per-minute is 8 METS, stair climbing at 120 steps-per-minute with a backpack weighing 40% of your body weight is 20 METS.

TABLE 5: YOUR AEROBIC HEART TRAINING RATE

Age	*YOUR MAXIMUM HEART RATE Beats Per Minute	BEGINNERS IN POOR SHAPE EXERCISE AT 60% OF THEIR MAXIMUM HEARTBEAT Beats Per Minute	Six Second Pulse Count	YOUR TARGET HEART RATE TRAINING RANGE (BETWEEN 70% AND 85% OF MAXIMUM BEATS PER MINUTE) Beats Per Minute	Six Second Pulse Count	TRY TO STAY AT YOUR TARGET HEART RATE (75% OF MAXIMUM BEATS PER MINUTE) Beats Per Minute	Six Second Pulse Count
20	200	120	12	140–170	14–17	150	15
25	195	117	12	137–166	14–17	146	15
30	190	114	11	133–162	13–16	142	14
35	185	111	11	130–157	13–16	139	14
40	180	108	11	126–153	13–15	135	14
45	175	105	11	123–149	12–15	131	13
50	170	102	10	119–145	12–15	127	13
55	165	99	10	116–140	12–14	124	12
60	160	96	10	112–136	11–14	120	12
65	155	93	9	109–132	11–13	116	12
70	150	90	9	105–128	11–13	112	11

*Your maximum heart rate: Exercise at least 15% below this rate.

The five Fitness/Workout Levels have a range of MET values. METS measure the intensity of the exercise and also refer to your body's ability to perform the exercise without tiring too fast. For example, if you are in poor to fair shape, you probably can work out continuously at a MET no higher than 5, and you will be in the 2-8 MET range for your Workouts. If you are in good shape (Level III), your MET range will be 8-12. The MET range at Level IV is 12-15, at Level V, 15-22.

METS are related to calories, too. Table 6 shows you how to compute the calories you burn exercising at a certain MET range, by your body weight.

TABLE 6: CONVERTING METS TO CALORIES OF EXERCISE

Determine the calorie and METS/value (intensity) of any walking exercise by using the two formulas and sets of tables listed below:

A. The METS formula

Compare your pulse rate with a known METS value to your pulse rate for an exercise for which you do not know the METS value. For example, level walking at 3 mph is a 4 METS activity which may raise your exercising heart rate to 120 beats per minute. If you walk faster so that your heart rate goes to 150 beats per minute, what will be the METS value of that new walking speed?

$$\frac{4 \text{ METS}}{120 \text{ pulse}} = \frac{N \text{ METS}}{150 \text{ pulse}}$$

simplify: $120 \times N = 4 \times 150$
N or the new METS value:

$$\frac{4 \times 150}{120} = 5 \text{ METS}$$

B. The Calories of Exercise formula

You can determine the number of calories you burned during a continuous exercise period by multiplying the METS value of the exercise by the METS Body Weight Factor listed below and by the number of exercise minutes. For example, if you exercise for 30 minutes at 5 METS and weigh 187 pounds, you compute your exercise calories as follows:

1.5 (The Mets Body Weight Factor) $\times$ 30 (minutes) $\times$ 5 (METS) = 225 calories.

YOUR BODY WEIGHT		YOUR METS BODY WEIGHT FACTOR	YOUR BODY WEIGHT		YOUR METS BODY WEIGHT FACTOR
Pounds	Kilos	Multiply By:	Pounds	Kilos	Multiply By:
55	25	0.5	156	71	1.25
60	27.27	0.53	160	72.73	1.28
66	30	0.57	165	75	1.32
70	31.82	0.6	170	77.27	1.36
77	35	0.64	176	80	1.41
80	36.36	0.66	180	81.82	1.44
88	40	0.71	187	85	1.5
90	40.91	0.72	190	86.36	1.53
95	43	0.75	198	90	1.58
99	45	0.78	200	90.91	1.61
100	45.44	0.79	209	95	1.67
105	47.73	0.83	215	97.73	1.71
110	50	0.875	220	100	1.75
115	52.27	0.93	225	102.27	1.79
120	54.55	0.92	231	105	1.83
121	55	0.97	240	109.09	1.91
125	57	1.0	242	110	1.93
130	59.09	1.04	245	111.36	1.95
132	60	1.06	251	114	2.0
140	63.64	1.12	253	115	2.03
143	65	1.15	260	118.18	2.07
150	68.18	1.2	264	120	2.11
154	70	1.24			

CHAPTER

1 The Pacewalk Workout

EVEN THOUGH YOU may never be able to walk or run a six-minute mile, you can still learn to walk fast enough to achieve the same cardiovascular benefits as jogging; without jogging's injuries. The secret is in your arms.

Pacewalking is fast cadenced walking with arm pumping. It is the basic aerobic walker's Workout—the walking equivalent of jogging or jogging in place. In this chapter you will learn how to build up your walking pace so that you can sustain 3.5 to 5.5 mph on the move and 120 to 180 steps per minute in place for at least 15 and up to 60 minutes. Most people can sustain a fast walking pace for one to two minutes, but it takes practice and the use of special techniques to reach the level of aerobic Pacewalking.

Pacewalking includes four walking speeds: slow (1 to 3 mph on the move or 30 to 90 steps per minute in place—spm); brisk (3 to 4 mph or 90 to 120 spm); fast (4 to 5.5 mph or 120 to 150 spm) and sprint (5.5 to 10 mph or 150 to 200 spm).

TABLE 7: Pacewalk MET Levels (Level Walking)

mph	spm	METS*	Exercise Calories per Hour**	For Fitness Levels:
1	30	1.5	100	I
1.5	40	2	150	
2	45	3	200	II
2.5	60	3.5	250	
3	90	4	300	III
3.5	100	5	360	
3.75	110	5.5	380	
4	120	6	400	
4.25	125	7	440	
4.5	130	7.5	480	
5	140	8	550	
5.5	150	9	650	
6	160	10	750	
6.5	165	11	850	
7	170	12	950	IV
7.5	175	13	1000	
8	180	14	1050	
9	190	15	1100	V
9.5	195	16	1200	
10	200	17	1300	

* Applicable to all persons
**Applicable to a person weighing 150 pounds (70kg)

TABLE 8: SPEED GOALS

	I	II	III	IV	V
Week # 1					
mph*	2	3	3.5	4.5	5.5
mm	30	20	17	13	10.9
spm	45	90	100	130	150
Week #2					
mph	2.25	3	3.5	4.5	5.5
mm	26.7	20	17	13	10.9
spm	55	90	100	130	150
Week #3					
mph	2.5	3.25	3.75	4.75	5.75
mm	24	18.5	16	12.6	10.4
spm	60	95	110	135	155
Week #4					
mph	2.75	3.25	4	5	6
mm	21.8	18.5	15	12	10
spm	75	95	120	140	160
Week #5					
mph	2.75	3.5	4.25	5.25	6.5
mm	21.8	17	14	11	9.2
spm	75	100	125	145	163
Week #6					
mph	3	3.5	4.5	5.5	7
mm	20	17	13	10.9	8.6
spm	90	100	130	150	170

*mph are miles per hour
mm are minute miles
spm are steps per minute

The four are part of a speed continuum you practice during each Pacewalk Workout. Set your goals for the speed gain you want to achieve each week over the six-week training period using Table 8. During the aerobic part of the Workout monitor your pulse and heart training rate at least once to see that your speed goal puts you in the aerobic heart training range (see p. 71).

Four new techniques are needed for the Pacewalk Workout:

Technique #9

The Arm Pumps

Make the arm swing you learned in the basic Walking Techniques section more dynamic by pumping from your forearms vigorously, instead of swinging your arms with just your shoulder muscles. Start pumping with your arms straight (slightly bent at the elbow). As you pump faster, bend your arms first at a 90-degree angle, then, as you pump even faster, at a 45-degree angle. Pump and swing your arms straight forward and straight back just as you did with the basic arm swings. Remember to keep your fists loosely clenched.

Practice the following series of low, medium, high, and overhead pumps, first with arms straight, then with arms bent. As you did with the arm swings, practice the arm pumps with cadence breathing. Pump as fast and as vigorously as you can.

Low Pumps (10 to 20 counts) Swing your arms forward at stomach height and back to the small of your back in a 45-degree arc.

Medium Pumps (20 counts) Swing your arms forward at chest height and back at a 90-degree angle.

High Pumps (20 counts) Swing your arms forward from your shoulders to head height and straight back as far (about 120 to 180 degrees) as is comfortable and practical for recovering to make the next forward swing.

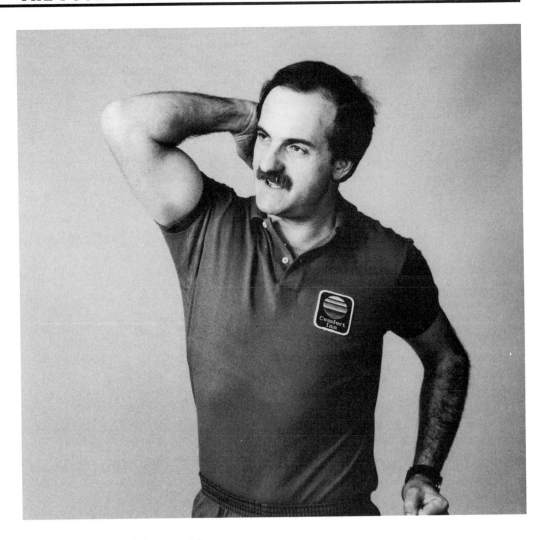

Overhead Pumps (20 counts) Swing your
arms forward over and behind your head
and back down to behind your back.

Arm Pump Calisthenics

Convert your arm pumping technique into an upper body calisthenic strengthening exercise by doing this additional series of arm pumps.

Crossover Pumps (20 counts) Swing each arm diagonally across your chest to the opposite shoulder and back again in a straight line to train your chest (pectoral) and shoulder muscles.

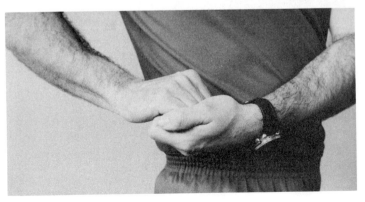

Cradle Pumps (20 counts) Clasp your fingers together and from the middle of your chest swing both arms to the right and back to the middle of your chest for 10 counts, then to the left and back to the middle of your chest for 10 counts. Turn your body and head in the direction of your arm swing.

Practicing the Arm Pumps in Place

As you master the arm pumps and accelerate your arms and legs into the aerobic pace range, use high/low combinations, i.e., high leg lifts with low arm pumps and low leg lifts with high arm pumps. Vary your routine by going from low to high and back down to low, all the time maintaining a steady pace. For example, do a straight low arm pump series with increasingly higher leg lifts.

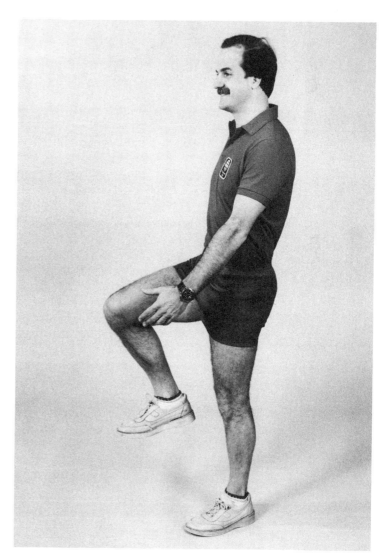

Straight Arm Slightly Bent at the Elbow

45-degree Bent Arm Pump. These are also
called "Sprinter's Pumps" because they are
just like the arm pumps of sprint runners.

45-degree Crossover Pumps. These are called
"Upper Cuts" because they are like the short
jabs of a boxer.

Walking Faults Corrected

If your shoulders rise and fall when you walk, your shoulders and upper back are probably not relaxed. Reduce the vigor of your arm pumping and do shoulder stretches like the Shoulder Shrugs and Windmill to improve your flexibility. The Cradle Pump, when practiced slowly, will also improve flexibility in the shoulders.

Don't swing your arms in an uncoordinated action. Reduce the pumping speed and practice controlled pumps in front of a mirror to make sure you are swinging your arms straight back and straight forward.

Bent Arm Pumps can be done just as easily walking in place as walking on the move, you just have to do quicker paced steps to keep up with the shorter arm swings.

Technique #10

The Stride Stretch Technique

To increase your walking speed you must first increase the length of each step or stride. To do this you need to extend your hip. In other words, let your hip follow through after the leg swings forward. This technique can add 8 inches or more to your stride length. Most walkers can't stretch their stride past 3 feet. With hip walking you'll be able to reach almost four feet. Using your hips more in walking reduces the rising and falling of your body and converts that vertical energy to horizontal energy. The more hip you put into your step, the more you will be working your buttocks and abdominal muscles.

Practice the Stride Stretch Technique first from the Basic Starting Position. Take one step forward, extending your leg as far as it will go. Then with your feet pointed in the direction of travel, take a great giant step forward, landing on your heel. Be sure your back foot remains pointed forward. Hold for 3 counts, then lift *forward* foot placing it an additional 3 to 5 inches further forward. Hold that position 3 to 5 seconds and withdraw your forward foot to the starting position. Perform the same exercise with the other foot. Repeat the Stride Stretch five times for each foot. In place, take two Stride Steps forward and two Stride Steps backward.

How the Walker Lengthens His Stride

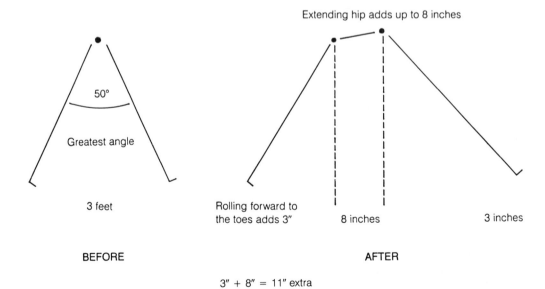

Now practice the Stride Stretch from the Stride Stance Position by bringing your rear leg forward and straightening it immediately after making ground contact. Then, step back and try it again. When the heel is about to strike, your leg should only be slightly bent at the knee. As the heel makes contact, immediately begin to straighten your leg. Repeat the exercise on each leg 5 counts.

When walking in place you can practice using your hips by raising them as you raise each leg. This is called "hip walking."

Walking Faults Corrected

If your stride is too short, your walking speed will be too slow and you will need extra steps to achieve your minimum Pacewalk speeds. To increase your stride, practice taking longer steps using your hips to follow through after your leg swings forward and doing stretching exercises (see p. 51) to improve your hip flexibility. If your stride is too long, your forward leg will look stiff and your rear leg will bend too soon. Correct this by increasing your step speed and shortening your stride length.

If your hips appear to be swaying from side to side, you are wasting energy. Correct this by moving your hips down and forward when your leg is completing its swing.

Straightening the Supporting Leg

Technique #11

In Technique #6, the Toe-off, you learned how to roll all the way up onto your toes before pushing off. Now you will learn to add even more forward drive to your toe-off and at the same time lengthen your stride for a faster walking speed.

Think of your supporting leg as a vaulting pole. Remember each of your legs becomes a supporting leg when its heel strikes the ground. At that point you should straighten the leg completely and bend it back slightly, locking the knee. Keep your supporting leg straight throughout the heel-toe roll, all the way to the toe-off. Your leg should be straightening itself as soon as it has cleared under your body and is getting ready to execute the heel strike.

By acting as a pole vault, your supporting leg will give you additional momentum and time to let your forward swinging leg take a longer stride. And it will prolong the thrust of the toe-off by keeping you in contact with the ground longer.

Practice walking in slow motion and stop after the toe-off to look back at your supporting leg to see if your toes are pointed in the direction of travel. Also, feel the knee locking after the heel strike so you will know that the leg has been straightened.

Practice taking each step straight-legged like a robot.

By prolonging the toe-off you can check and correct any bend in your leg. When I practice this technique, I picture myself ice skating, making the long-delayed thrusting action that allows you to glide on the ice before moving the next leg forward.

In-Place Walking

When lifting your legs for in-place walking be sure to straighten your supporting leg right after the forefoot strikes by purposefully bending back your knee as your foot rolls back to the heel. Straightening the supporting leg is an important technique to apply during all the Workouts, so practice it well.

Walking Faults Corrected

If your body rises and falls while you are walking, your stride length may be too short for your increased speed. Slow down and concentrate on lengthening your stride by straightening the supporting leg. Also, practice stretching exercises to improve your hip and ankle flexibility.

The Sprintwalk Technique

The Sprintwalk combines a wider stride and more rapid leg movement, with emphasis on the latter.

To learn to walk faster, you need to practice moving your legs faster over short distances and short time frames. Gradually you can build up the time and distance of your all-out fast pace. Increase your step rate by increasing the power of your forward driving or upward driving leg. Do this by increasing your leg strength which will also promote hip flexibility. You have to practice moving your legs faster.

In-Place Sprintwalk Exercise— The Shuffle Step

The shuffle step is, simply, sprintwalking in place, the only difference is that you can shuffle step sideways and forward and back in a small area. To shuffle step walk as fast as you can, moving your legs up and down about 2 to 5 inches off the ground with each step. Remember to keep one foot on the ground. Don't start jogging. Sprintwalking in place is different from "on the move" sprintwalking because you make contact with the ball of your foot rather than the heel. Then you roll back to your heel on the outer edge of your foot and forward again before toeing off.

At first do short bursts of shuffle stepping in place (5 to 10 seconds in duration). Build up your shuffle step duration time by using the interval-training schedule in Tables 13 and 14. Advanced walkers can start at the 10 to 20 second range and build from there.

Determine your speed for Pacewalk aerobic routines by taking 60% of your shuffle-step pace: count the number of steps in 15 seconds. Multiply by 4 to get your maximum steps per minute. Your aerobic Pacewalk rate is 75% of that.

Practice the Sprintwalk in place with the up and down shuffle step at first. Vary the exercise with front and back shuffle steps, crossover, and side to side steps. These are steps you'll be using in the Dancewalk routines in Chapter 4.

Sprintwalk on the Move

In this technique you will substitute a wider stride for a less rapid step rate. The maximum speed you will probably achieve is 200 steps per minute (spm) with a four foot stride. That means a six-minute mile. Over distances of 100 to 880 yards, you may be able to go faster, but this will depend on your strength and natural leg speed. For fitness, you should be satisfied

TABLE 9: CADENCE COUNTING CHART

Paces (Steps) per Minute	Paces (Steps) per Second	Speed in MPH	Cadence Count	Paces (Steps) per 6 Seconds
60	1 step sec.	2.5	1 and (1 sec)	6
80	4 steps/3 sec.	2.75	1,2,3,4	8
90	3 steps/2 sec.	3.0	1,2 and (2 sec)	9
100	5 steps/3 sec.	3.5	1,2,3, and 1,2,3, (3 sec)	10
110	2/sec	3.75	1,2,1,2 (2 sec)	12
120	7/ 3 sec	4.0	1,2,3,4,5,6,7 (3 sec)	14
140	5/2 sec.	5.0	1,2,3,4, and (2 sec)	15
150	8/3 sec	5.5	1,2; 1,2; 1,2, (3 sec)	16
160	3/sec	6.0	1,2,3; 1,2,3; 1,2,3, (3 sec)	18
180	10/3 sec	8.0	1,2,3,4,5; 1,2,3,4,5, (2 sec)	20
200		10.0		

with the 130 to 180 steps-per-minute range (see Table 14, p. 99).

Now that you have learned the special techniques and movements needed for the Pacewalk Workout, there are just two more things you need to know.

Rest Intervals

During the Pacewalk you will be practicing what is known as rest or slow walk intervals. These are short periods (about 10 to 30 seconds) when you walk as fast as you can, then rest or walk slowly. If you monitor your pulse during the rest intervals, you will notice that as you become more conditioned the gaps between your resting pulse and your Workout pulse will diminish as will the time it takes to return to your working pulse rate from the rest period.

Counting Cadences

In the beginning count your walking cadences out loud, exhaling on the count and inhaling before you count. For faster paces exhale and inhale every two counts. Use a six-second count method. When one count equals one step you can multiply the number of counts by 10 to get steps per minute. You will have to alter your cadence as you alter your speed. For example, at 120 spm you will be taking two steps every second and you will have to count 1,2 every second. At 180 spm, you will have to count three steps a second—1,2,3. The slower 60 steps per minute are counted 1 and 2 and, etc.

The Pacewalk Workout

The Warm-Up Pacewalk
(2 to 5 minutes)

On the Move

Walk briskly at a 3 to 3.5 mile-per-hour (90 to 100 spm) pace. Take a wide stride with each step. Beginners should walk for two minutes (90 counts); advanced for five minutes (100 counts). As you walk use the following series of straight arm pumps as your upper body warm-up exercise:

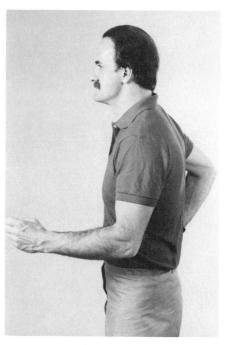

Minute One: Straight Arm Low Pumps—Chest Height (90 to 100 counts)

Minute Two: Straight Arm Medium Pumps—Head Height (90 to 100 Counts) (Advanced walkers continue with minutes three through five)

Minute Three: Straight Arm Overhead Pumps (90 to 100 counts)

Minute Four: Bent Arm (90-degrees) Low Pumps (90 to 100 counts)

Minute Five: Bent Arm (90-degrees) Medium Pumps (90 to 100 counts)
Note: Use the 6-second cadence count table on page 90 for the pace counts that will regulate your speed.

In Place

Walk briskly at 80 (beginners) to 100 (advanced) steps per minute for 2 to 5 minutes using the following combination of arm and leg movements. Note that in-place Pacewalkers practice a wider variety of arm and leg movements to make the exercise in a small place more interesting.

Minute One: Straight Arms with Up and Down Leg Lifts (Do 20 to 25 counts of each arm/leg movement.)

Arms		*Legs*
Straight Arm Low Pumps	with	Medium Leg Lifts

Straight Arm Medium Pumps	with	Medium Leg Lifts
Straight Arm High Pumps	with	High Leg Lifts
Straight Arm Overhead Pumps	with	Shuffle Steps

Minute Two: Three Steps Forward and Back (Do 20 to 25 counts of each arm/leg movement.)

Arms		*Legs*
Straight Arm Low Pumps	with	3 Shuffle Steps Forward
Straight Arm Medium Pumps	with	3 Shuffle Steps Back
Straight Arm High Pumps	with	3 Shuffle Steps Back
Straight Arm Overhead Pumps	with	3 Up and Down Leg Lifts

(Advanced walkers continue with minutes three through five.)

Minute Three: Bent Arms with Up and Down Leg Lifts (Do 15 to 20 counts of each arm/leg movement.)

Arms		*Legs*
Bent Arm (90-degrees)	with	Leg Lifts
Low Pumps	with	High Leg Lifts
Medium Pumps	with	High Leg Lifts
High Pumps	with	Medium Leg Lifts
Overhead Pumps	with	Shuffle Steps

Minute Four: L Steps: This routine will walk you in the shape of an L. Combine two L routines to walk in the shape of a box.

Arms	*Legs*
Bent Arm Pumps	Shuffle L steps
(45-degrees)	(45 steps in total)
Low	3 Steps Forward
	3 Up and Down Leg Lifts
	3 Steps Back
	3 Up and Down Leg Lifts
Medium	3 Crossover Steps Left
	3 Up and Down Leg Lifts
High	3 Crossover Steps Right
	3 Up and Down Leg Lifts
Overhead	3 Steps Forward
	3 Up and Down Leg Lifts
	3 Crossover Steps Left
	3 Up and Down Leg Lifts
	3 Steps Backward
	3 Up and Down Leg Lifts
	3 Crossover Steps Right

Minute Five: Multiple Arms and Legs (Do 15 to 20 counts of
each arm/leg movement.)

Arms		*Legs*
Crossover Pumps	with	Up and Down Leg Lifts
Straight Arm Pumps	with	3 Steps Forward and Back
Bent Arm Pumps	with	Crossover Steps Right and Left
Cradle Pumps, Left and Right	with	Crossover Steps Right and Left
Overhead Bent Arm Pumps	with	Up and Down Leg Lifts

Pacewalk Warm-Up Stretching

(5 to 10 minutes)

The purpose of Pacewalk stretching is to increase the range and
speed of your leg and arm movements.

The Basic Four

1. The Calf and Achilles Tendon Stretch (see p. 35)

2. The Quadriceps and Ankle Stretch (see p. 36)

3. The Hamstring Stretch (see p. 37)

4. The Flying Lunge Stretch (see p. 39)

Specifically for the Pacewalk Workout

1. Shoulders: Windmills (Single and Double Arms) (see p. 42)

2. Hips: Hip Stretch (see p. 51), Standing Back and Hip Stretch
   (see p. 57), Standing Hip Stretch (see p. 53)

3. Upper Legs: Standing Quadricep and Ankle Stretch (see Basic
   Four)

4. Ankles: Heel-Walk Exercises (see p. 23), Toe-Off Exercises
   (see p. 26), Heel-Toe Roll Exercises (see p. 25)

Pacewalk Techniques and Calisthenics

(5 to 10 minutes)

Techniques are not something you learn all at once. You need to keep practicing and refining them as you increase your walking speed. Continue to devote 5 to 10 minutes of every Workout to practicing techniques. Vary and build your walking speed by monitoring your cadences, thereby controlling your step rate.

Use the basic Walking Techniques (numbers 1-8) and then do these special Pacewalking Techniques:

> Technique Number Nine: The Arm Pumps
> Technique Number Ten: The Stride Stretch
> Technique Number Eleven: Straightening the Supporting Leg
> Technique Number Twelve: Sprintwalking

Starter Aerobics/Mileage Program

Beginners: For those of you in poor physical condition, now is the time to build up your walking miles. Consider your Starter Program as the beginning of your basic Daily Walking program for weight control and relaxation. Start slowly at 60 spm, a 24-minute mile or 2.5 mph. Concentrate on one technique at a time (proper posture, for example, or the toe-off). Once you have perfected a technique, incorporate it into your Daily Walking session. In-place walkers should vary this walking session, using three steps forward and three steps backward.

TABLE 10: BEGINNER'S STARTER PROGRAM
Building Up Distance and Walking Speed While Practicing Techniques

Week #	Mileage/Day	Frequency per Week	Time per Session	Total Weekly Mileage	Minutes per Mile	MPH	SPM
1	1	3	40	6	24	2.5	60
2	2	4	40	8	24	2.5	60
3	2.5	4	60	10	24	3.0	60
4	3.0	4	60	12	20	3.0	90
5	3.0	4	60	12	20	3.0	90
6	4.0	4	80	14	20	3.0	90

TABLE 11: ADVANCED STARTER PROGRAM
Building Up Distance and Walking Speed While Practicing Techniques

Week #	Mileage/Day	Frequency per Week	Time per Session	Total Weekly Mileage	SPEED		
					Minutes per Mile	MPH	SPM
1	2	3	40	6	20	3	90
2	2.5	3	50	7.5	20	3	90
3	3	3	60	9	20	3	90
4	3.5	4	60	12	17	3.5	100
5	3.5	4	60	14	17	3.5	100
6	4	5	60	20	15	4	100

Advanced: Those of you in good physical condition still need to develop your walking muscles and practice your walking techniques while gradually increasing your walking speed. Advanced walkers should consider the Starter Program as the beginning of the basic Daily Walking program. Concentrate on individual techniques (proper posture, cadenced breathing, outer edge roll, etc.) and, once you perfect them, integrate them into your Daily Walking sessions.

Pacewalking Aerobics
(15 to 30 minutes)

Your aerobic pace is the pace you can comfortably sustain for 15 minutes without breathing too heavily. For beginning Pacewalkers the maximum aerobic pace lies between a 17- and 14-minute mile. For advanced Pacewalkers it is between a 14- and 10-minute mile. Take your six-second pulse rate and refer to Table 12 on page 98 to determine your starting aerobic pace.

The Pacewalk aerobics routine that follows contains a continuous walking routine and a speed interval routine. The first is to train you for endurance in the aerobic training range, and the second is to help you increase your walking speed for aerobic training.

You should not practice a full interval training session until you are able to sustain a 16-minute-mile pace (3.75 mph or 110 spm) for 15 minutes.

Aerobic Pacewalking Routines

Practice the same arm movements and follow the same pacing routines for both in-place and on-the-move Pacewalking. You will be spending the 15 to 30 minute aerobic session doing four pacing routines and a cool-down. (There is a fifth, Sprintwalking routine, for advanced walkers.)

Routine #1: The Wind-Up (1 minute) Do 90 to 100 counts of straight arm low pumps while walking briskly.

Routine #2: Stepping Up the Pace (3 minutes) Accelerate your walking pace in three intervals, each interval increasing the speed by 10 steps per minute.

Minute	Beginners	Advanced
Minute One	100 spm	110 spm
Minute Two	110 spm	120 spm
Minute Three	120 spm	130 spm

As you become more fit your walking speed must start at a higher rate and accelerate from there (see Table 3: Walking Speed, p. 33).

In-place walkers and on-the-move walkers should practice Minutes Two through Four of their arm/leg routines (from the warmup for Pacewalk, p. 92), accelerating the pace at the beginning of each minute.

Routine #3: Brisk or Fast Steady Pace (10-15 minutes) This is the period when you sustain your walking pace so that your heart is beating in the training zone while you exercise. Beginners should be in the 100 to 130 steps per minute range, advanced walkers in the 120-150 spm range. If you have problems maintaining your target pace, drop your speed until you have recuperated and then accelerate again into your pacing zone.*

Start the period with Minute Five Routines from the Warm-Up Walk, then do the following Aerobic Pacewalking Routines:

On the Move To keep the aerobic pace, advanced walkers will have to use bent arm pumps almost exclusively through the rest of this routine. Practice bent arm pumps front and back, alternating the 90-degree and 45-degree pumps every other minute,

---

*If you have a problem reaching the aerobic heart training zone wear a waist belt or weight loaded backpack.

while concentrating on maintaining a wide stride. Instead of practicing a variety of arm movements, concentrate on only these two. Pay attention to each one of your walking techniques separately as you maintain a steady pace. For example, concentrate on holding proper posture, your heel strike, your outer edge roll, straightening your supporting leg, parallel arm and leg motion, synchronized cadence breathing, and a straight, forward toe-off.

In Place Pacewalkers in place should use a variety of arm and leg movements, repeating the in-place stepping routine (see p. 91) in two or three sets of five minutes each. Once the stepping and arm routines become second nature, concentrate on applying and refining proper walking techniques to your aerobic routine. (Reread the walking techniques chapter to be sure you are doing all the smaller movements correctly.) As you grow stronger, accelerate your pace and use higher leg and arm swings. Practice holding proper posture and concentrate on each step and arm movement separately, reviewing, correcting and refining it in your mind as you do it.

Routine #4: Interval Training (2-5 minutes) This is the portion of your Workout when you practice speed work using interval training. In-place walkers should concentrate on pure up and down leg speed, trying to extend the duration of your highest leg speed. On-the-Move walkers should practice Sprintwalks at maximum speed and try (over the six-week training period) to increase the Sprintwalk distance from 100 to 440 yards (beginners) or from 440 to 880 yards (advanced). Beginners should not do the Sprintwalking routines until they have reached Level III fitness. If you are below Level III, continue to practice continuous walking or proceed to the Cool-Down section, skipping the interval training period.

Sprintwalkers in place should do the interval training with 90- or 45-degree uppercuts and shuffle steps or medium leg lifts.

Sprintwalkers on the move should also use 90- or 45-degree upper cuts, but should continue to maintain a wide stepping stride. Table 12 on page 98 will translate the steps per minute into minute miles for the Sprintwalkers on the move.

Routine #5: Sprintwalk Interval Training (Advanced Walkers) After completing Routine #4, advanced walkers should practice sprintwalk interval training for another one-minute period.

Sprintwalk #1:
Sprintwalk at 140 spm.
Sprintwalk #2:
Sprintwalk at 150 spm.
Sprintwalk #3:
Sprintwalk as fast as you can for one minute and count the number of steps you took. Note your score.

At the end of the Sprintwalks, return to your continuous Pacewalking training speed (see p. 94) until your pulse rate stabilizes *within* your heart training zone.

Practice your Sprintwalk in place with up and down leg lifts of medium height and shuffle steps (see p. 89). The Sprintwalk speed range is 130 to 200 steps per minute. Walk your maximum speed and try to extend the time you can sustain it from five seconds to five minutes. Build to that higher range by using rest intervals or slow walk intervals. Use shuffle steps and short bent arm pumps for the fastest arm/leg repetitions.

TABLE 12: AEROBIC PACEWALKING PACE (SPEED) LEVELS

Level	MPH	Steps per Minute	Minute Miles	METS Value
Level I Poor/Easy Intensity	2–3	45–90	20–30	3–4
Level II Fair/Moderate Intensity	3–3.5	90–100	17–20	4–5
Level III Good/Brisk Intensity	3.5–4.5	100–300	13–17	5–8
Level IV Very Good/ Vigorous (Fast)	4.5–5.5	130–150	11–13	8–15
Level V Excellent/High Intensity (Sprint)	5.5–10	150–200	6–11	15–17

TABLE 13: SPEED OVER TIME INTERVAL TRAINING

Practice Sprintwalking (5–60 seconds). Record your fastest steps per minute rate in the last two columns.

Week #	Sprintwalk Speed Over Time				Fastest on the Move	Fastest in place
	Duration (Seconds)	Rest (Seconds)	Frequency per Session	Factor		
Beginner						
1	5	5–10	10	× 10		
2	10	10–20	10	× 6		
3	15	15–30	10	× 4		
Advanced						
4	20	20–30	5	× 3		
5	30	30–60	5	× 2		
6	60	60–120	5	× 1		

TABLE 14: SPRINTWALK SPEED OVER DISTANCE (ON THE MOVE)

Week #	Distance	Pace (spm)	Repetitions	Record Maximum Speed
1	100 yards	150–180	5–10	
2	220 yards	130–150	5–10	
3	220 yards	130–150	5–10	
4	440 yards	130–150	5–10	
5	440 yards	130–150	5–10	
6	880 yards	130–150	2–4	
Levels IV and V				
7	550 yards	130–150	2–4	
8	880 yards	130–140	2–4	
9	550 yards	140–150	2–4	
10	880 yards	135–150	2–4	
11	1.0 mile	130–140	2	
12	.75 mile	150	2	
13	1.0 mile	140	2	
14	.75 mile	155	2	
15	.75 mile	145	2	
16	1.0 mile	155	2	
17	.5 mile	155	3	
18	1.5 miles	155	1	
19	.5 mile	155	3	
20	1.5 miles	160	2	

The Pacewalk Cool-Down

(2-5 minutes)

Reduce your pace until you reach 60 to 90 steps per minute.

Minutes 1 and 2: Decelerate to 100-120 spm.

Minutes 3 and 4: Decelerate to 90-100 spm.

Minute 5: Decelerate to 60-90 spm.

Note: You will use this Cool-Down after all your aerobic Walking Workouts. You can extend the time of your Cool-Down, but do not shorten it or stop your Workout suddenly.

Cool-Down Stretches

Stretch body areas which are tight using the appropriate stretch listed in the Pacewalk Warm-Up Stretching (see p. 93). Then practice the following stretches which are also designed to relax you.

Hang Over Stretch (p. 56)
Inverted V (p. 57)
Hip and Back Relaxer (p. 59)
Groin and Lower Back Stretch (p. 60)
Overhead Leg Stretch (p. 62)
Lying Down Neck Stretch (p. 63)

The Weightwalk Workout

THE WEIGHTWALK WORKOUT is a way to slow your exercising to a hiking or recreational walker's pace while still training aerobically. You trade speed for a slower pace with weight resistance. The Weightwalk Workout is an aerobic and weight training routine. Weight loaded routines can be done at a slow pace and still produce the cardiovascular training effect.

The Weightwalk Workout involves a combination of weight load and speed increases as well as increases in the range of motion of the legs and arms. You will pump your arms faster and lift your legs higher, thus training more limb and trunk muscles. At the same time you will be increasing your flexibility.

Note: Weight loaded walking can produce injuries to joints if you overload too much on one joint. Carefully follow the weight loading guidelines and be sure to do the stretching exercises before and after the Weightwalk Workout. Weightwalking is generally considered a more advanced exercise routine, so it is best not to start

weight loading until you have done six weeks of Walking Workouts without weights. For this reason the beginner's Weightwalk Workout is a weight-free workout, using greater arm and leg motion and your own body weight. (Your limbs are already weighted down with muscle, bone and fat. There's enough weight there to work with for an untrained body.)

If you are in good shape, but not skilled in walking movements, begin practicing the Weightwalk techniques with one or two pound weights on your ankles or wrists.

You may have already done some weight loaded walking with a backpack in order to raise your pulse rate into the training zone during the Pacewalk Workout. If you've done any backpacking or carried a heavy bag of groceries, you probably have discovered already that your heart rate goes up if you increase the workload without increasing your walking speed. Your heart rate goes up even more when you weight load your arms and legs. In fact, if you put the weight on

TABLE 15: PROGRESSIVE WEIGHT LOADING SCHEDULE
(If you are at level I or II do these exercises without weights or with 1 lb. weights at most.)

PART I

Walking Speed Arm/Leg Repetitions	Walking Distance (miles per session)		Hand Weights (in pounds)			In Combination with hands and trunk			Ankle Weights (in pounds)		
			III	IV	V	III	IV	V	III	IV	V
Week #1 mph = 1–2	.5	Men	1	1	3						
spm = 30–45		Women	½	½	1						
Week #2 mph = 1.5–2.5	.5–1	Men	1	2	3						
spm = 40–60		Women	½	1	1						
Week #3 mph = 1.5–3	.75–1.25	Men	1	2	3	5	5	5	1	1	1
spm = 40–90		Women	1	1	1	0	0	5	½	½	½
Week #4 mph = 2–3.5	1–2	Men	1	2	3	5	5	5	1	1	1½
spm = 45–100		Women	1	1	1	5	5	5	½	¾	1
Week #5 mph = 2.5–3.0	1.5–2.5	Men	1	2	3	5	5	5	1	1½	2
spm = 60–90		Women	1	1	1	5	5	5	¾	1	1¼
Week #6 mph = 2.5–3.0	2–3	Men	2	3	4	6	8	10	1¼	2	2½
spm = 60–90		Women	2	3	3	5	6	7	¾	1	1½
Advanced Training											
Week #1 mph = 2.5–3.0	2–3	Men	3	4	5	7	8	12	1½	2	2¾
spm = 60–90		Women	2	3	3	5	6	7	¾	1	1½
Week #2 mph = 2.5–3.0	2.5–3.5	Men	4	5	6	8	9	15	1½	2	3¼
spm = 60–90		Women	3	5	5	6	7	8	¾	1	1½
Week #3 mph = 2.5–4.0	2.5–3.5	Men	5	6	8	9	10	18	1½	2¼	3½
spm = 60–120		Women	3	5	5	6	7	8	¾	1	1½
Week #4 mph = 2.5–4.0	3–4	Men	6	7	10	10	12	20	1¾	2½	4
spm = 60–120		Women	4	6	7	7	8	12	1	1½	2
Week #5 mph = 3.0–4.0	3–4	Men	7	8	12	11	13	22	1¾	2½	4½
spm = 90–120		Women	4	7	8	7	9	15	1½	1¾	2½
Week #6 mph = 3.5–5.0	4–5	Men	8	10	15	12	15	25	2	3	5
spm = 100–140		Women	5	8	10	8	10	15	1½	2	3

Weight Loading Routines

During the calisthenics portion of your workout use the weights recommended here. You can use heavier weights if you are a body builder. However, you should return to the charts recommendations in all combined movements such as the Weightwalk aerobic routines. Practice Weightwalking routines as aerobic and muscle building routines and combine them with Pace and Climbwalking. When using these routines for muscle development and toning be sure to pay attention to the rule of specificity in skeletal muscle development. You should train specific muscles in the same way you would do weight training in a gym.

Note that the weight tables assume a 180-pound man and a 130-pound woman. The age bracket is 30 to 50 years old. If you are younger or older, lighter or heavier, you should adjust the weight up or down. Remember not to exceed 40% of total body weight in the total poundage used. If a particular weight load addition is too heavy—you experience soreness the day after—drop back by half of that increase and work your way back up from there.

For muscle toning concentrate on hand and ankle weights. If you are interested in building your upper body, increase weights from 1 to 15 pounds on each hand. Use arm-pump swings with all hand weights over two pounds. Ankle weights should generally not go any higher than five pounds on each ankle (always count boot weight). Trunk loading in combination with hand and ankles should not exceed 40 pounds even for 200-pound persons. Remember that weight on swinging arms is worth five times what it is on the trunk and worth seven times the trunk weight for the legs.

PART II WEIGHTWALKING METS LEVELS

METS Value	Hand or Ankle Weight	Total % of Body Weight	Low Pump or Leg Lift	Mid Pump or Leg Lift	High Pump or Leg Lift	Torso Bend
Level I (2–5 METS)	*1 Pound Limit*					
2	no weight				45 spm	
3	no weight				60 spm	
	1 lb		100 spm			
3.5	1 lb		120 spm			
4						
5	1 lb			120 spm	100 spm	
		max. 10 % of body weight				
Level II (5–8 METS)	*2 Pound Limit*					
5	1 lb					
	2 lbs					
6	1 lb					
	2 lbs			100 spm		
7	1 lb			140 spm	120 spm	
	1 lb					Hoe Down/120 spm
	2 lbs			120 spm		
8	1 lb				140 spm	
	2 lbs			150 spm		
		20 % of body weight				

Table 15 (continued)

METS Value	Hand or Ankle Weight	Total % of Body Weight	Low Pump or Leg Lift	Mid Pump or Leg Lift	High Pump or Leg Lift	Torso Bend
Level III (8–12 METS)		*Weight Limit Women: 5 lbs; Men: 8 lbs*				
8	5 lbs		130 spm			
9	2 lbs			160 spm		
	3 lbs			140 spm		
10	no weight				150 spm	
	1 lb			200 spm	120 spm	
11	2 lbs			200 spm		
12	2 lbs			200 spm	150 spm	
		20–30% of body weight				
Level IV (12–15 METS)		*Weight Limit Women: 8 lbs; Men: 10 lbs*				
13	1 lb				160 spm	
	3 lbs				140 spm	
	5 lbs			150 spm	120 spm	
	2 lbs				150 spm	
	10 lbs			100 spm		
	15 lbs		150 spm			
14	4 lbs			200 spm		
	3 lbs				150 spm	
15	4 lbs				150 spm	
Level V (17–22 METS)		*Weight Limit Women: 15 lbs; Men: 25 lbs*				
16–17	5 lbs				150 spm	
	8 lbs				120 spm	
19–22	10 lbs			120 spm		
	15 lbs			100 spm		

your arms or legs instead of your trunk, it enhances the exercise value by five and seven times, respectively. (That is, one pound of weight in your hands is worth five on your back, one pound strapped to your foot or ankle is worth seven on your back.) This is because your arms and legs work harder during walking than your trunk.

Some Talk About Muscles

With the Weightwalk Workout you will become more familiar with your different body parts and you will begin to feel how certain movements work certain areas of your body. This "body consciousness" will eventually enable you to direct your movements to work specific muscles that may be weaker or need more toning and development than others. Following are descriptions of the muscles you use in various walking movements.

Trapezius Muscles (Upper Back Muscles) These help pull your shoulders back for maintaining proper posture. They also pull your arm over your head, as when you do the double overhead arm pump.

Deltoids (On top of the Shoulder Joints) The Deltoids pull the arm forward and backward in the arm swing.

Rhomboids (Upper Back Muscles) These muscles are located between the shoulder blades and stabilize and rotate them.

Biceps (Upper Arm Muscles) These two-headed muscles go from the elbow to the top of the arm where it joins the shoulder. You bend and straighten your arm with the biceps as you do the bent arm pump and the bicep curl.

Triceps (Back of Upper Arm Muscles) These three-headed muscles go from the shoulder to the elbow. You unbend your bent arm using the triceps (as in the tricep extension and back swing of the arm pump).

Pectorals (Fan-Shaped Front Chest Muscles) The pectorals pull your arms across your body and also swing them in most directions.

Spinal Erectors (Muscles of the Lower Back) These muscles help maintain your posture and raise and lower your body during the Hoe Downs.

Abdominals (Front and Side Wall Muscles of Trunk) You curl and twist your trunk using these.

Obliques (Side of Body Muscles) The oblique muscles help the body maintain correct posture while walking and they help you swing your leg forward. They also are used to twist the body front and back and from side to side during cross-over swings.

Hip Adductors (Inner and Outer Thigh Muscles) These muscles assist your legs in making crossover and side steps.

Hip Flexors (Front of Hip Muscles) These help swing the leg under the body and then forward.

Quadriceps (Front of Thigh Muscles) The quadriceps straighten the leg and bend the knee.

Quadratus Lumborum These muscles extend from the lower ribs to the pelvis posteriorly. They elevate the hip during hip walking.

Hamstrings (Rear of Thigh Muscles) The hamstrings help push the body upward and forward (the rear leg drive). The calf muscles assist the hamstrings with the final part of the rear leg drive.

Calf Muscles-Soleus Group (Back of Lower Leg) These are used to roll the foot forward in the heel-toe roll and also to toe-off in the rear leg drive.

Calf Muscle-Gastrocnemius (Back of Lower Leg) This muscle straightens your knee pulling the foot up and the leg forward under your body during the leg swing.

Peroneus Longus (Outside of Lower Leg) This muscle runs along the outside of your lower leg. It flexes your foot downward (after the toe-off) and also turns your foot outward during the outer edge roll.

Extensor or Shin Muscles (Front of Lower Leg) These are used to pull the lower leg under the body and to pull the foot upward prior to the heel strike.

Special Weightwalk Movements and Steps

As with the Pacewalk Workout, there are some new movements and steps you need to learn before beginning the Weightwalk Workout. By using weights you increase the resistance against your body while doing walking movements, in other words, your body has to do more work. You achieve even greater resistance by working your arms and legs in a higher and greater range of motion. Higher arm swings and leg lifts make your muscles work harder to overcome gravity.

The following is a series of weight loaded arm pumps and leg lifts used in the Weightwalk Workout. Practice each step and arm movement as a calisthenic strengthening exercise.

Weight Loaded Arm Pump Series

There are two types of arm pumps, the Weightwalk Pump and the Curl. These arm pumps are similar to those used in the Pacewalk Workout except that you bend and straighten your arms at the elbow like a bicep curl while pumping them back and forth in short swinging arcs of 45 degrees or less. Using these short swinging arcs with all your Weightwalk arm pumps in place will enable you to pump faster. You can use both short and long swinging arm pumps when you practice Weightwalking on the move.

Weight Loaded Straight Arm Pumps
Keeping your arms straight but slightly bent at the elbow, pump them with weights in your hands or on your wrists. Be sure to keep your head erect and your shoulders back. Breathe rhythmically with each swing, using the 2- or 4-count breathing cadence. Practice pumping each arm for 12 to 20 counts.

Note: It is not only the height at which you pump that is important, but also the length of the arc through which your arm swings.

Low Pumps Straight forward chest height.

High Pumps Shoulder to head height.

Overhead Pumps Overhead and straight back as far as your arms will comfortably go.

Weight Loaded Crossover Pumps Instead of pumping back and forth, pump your arms across your body to the opposite side. Practice each of the following crossover pumps for 12 to 20 counts.

Crossover Pumps (Scissors) Chest height to opposite shoulder.

Your arms serve as weights when you do the weightwalk without weights.

Crossover Pumps with Bent Arm (45 degrees) Head height to opposite ear.

Weight Loaded Bent Arm Pumps and Curls Repeat the same motions you used in the straight arm pumps but with your arms bent at 90 degrees first, then at 45 degrees. Be sure to pump your arms straight back and straight forward. Do each pump for 12 to 20 counts.

Crossover Pumps Chest height, across chest.

90-degree Pump and Curl Pump your weight loaded arms shoulder high and straight back as far as they will comfortably go. In-place walkers add curl to the pump.

45-degree Pump: Uppercut.
Chest High Uppercuts
Pump your arms at chest height back and forth.

Overhead Uppercuts (45 degrees)
Pump your arms shoulder height, over, and in back of head, then back again.

Double Arms:

90-degree-Shoulder High With both arms bent at a 90-degree angle, pump them in parallel fashion from shoulder height, straight back and return to shoulder height again for 12 to 20 counts.

Crossover Pumps Can be done with or without weights.

45-degree-Overhead With both arms bent at a 45-degree angle, pump them parallel to each other from shoulder height, overhead and back again for 12 to 20 counts.

Straight Arm Raises Straight arm raises use straight arm pumps to train your shoulder muscles. Practice each raising movement as a calisthenic exercise for 10 to 20 counts.

Side Arm Raises Raise both arms out to the sides, shoulder high, and lower them to the starting position.

Front Arm Raises Raise both arms palms
down in front of you, shoulder high, and
lower them slowly to starting position.

Weight Loaded Shrugs With weighted arms hanging at your sides, palms turned inward, lift shoulders up and let them down in a slow motion for 6 to 12 counts.

Double Arm Presses With your palms turned away from you, do the following presses. Press your weights straight up until the arms are straightened and bring them down again. Repeat each press for 12 to 20 counts.

Chest Presses Press straight up from a chest high position until arms are fully straightened. Slowly lower the weights to the starting position.

Front Shoulder Presses Press straight up from a shoulder high position until arms are fully straightened. Slowly lower weights to the starting position.

Overhead Cradle Swing from just below your chest to the back of your head and return again. Repeat for 12 to 20 counts.

Cradle Arm Pumps Instead of clasping your fingers together as you do in weight-free cradle pumps, hold your weights together for these weight-loaded cradle pumps. (If you use wrist weights, you can, of course, clasp your fingers together as you do for the regular cradle pumps.)

Back Shoulder Presses Press arms straight up from behind the head at shoulder height. Return slowly to the starting position.

Side Cradle Swing your arms from mid-stomach to the side and back. Repeat left side for 12 to 20 counts, then right side for 12 to 20 counts.

Then, hold your hands overhead, swinging your arms from shoulder to shoulder. Swing left with the left crossover step, swing right with the right side step, and so forth.

Arm Curls and Extensions

Bicep Curls from the Sides With arms at sides, palms facing forward, alternately curl each arm up to your shoulder and slowly lower it back down to the starting position. Repeat each arm for 12 to 20 counts.

Bicep Curls from Elbows, Shoulder High With both arms extended in front of you, curl each arm alternately to the top of the shoulder and extend it back again. Repeat each arm for 12 to 20 counts.

Tricep Extensions—Single Arms With body and arms bent at a 90-degree angle and upper arm parallel to your body, extend lower part of your arm up so that it is fully extended and return it again to the bent arm position. Repeat for 12 to 20 counts.

Bent Arm Flyes—Double or Single Arms

Breast Beaters With arms stretched out at shoulder height and palms turned away from your body, bring both your hands into your chest and back out again. (You can alternate arms or swing them simultaneously.) Repeat for 12 to 20 counts.

Elbow Flyes With arms stretched out from your shoulders, elbows bent at 90-degrees, bring elbows together into the chest and back out again. Repeat for 12 to 20 counts.

The March Step Series

The march step series involves walking with increasingly higher leg lifts. The march step is not a quick one like the shuffle step, but its pace can be quickened with practice. With the march step you always land on your forefoot, not on your heel, even when on the move.

March Stepping in Place Practice good walking techniques while marching by pointing your toes in the direction of travel. Remember to land on the ball of your foot first. Before lifting your foot, roll up on the outer edge of your foot keeping both feet parallel and toes pointed forward. Push off with your toes. Practice marching in place, stepping with each leg for 30 to 60 counts. Use the different march steps which follow:

The Low-Step March Feet are raised 3 to 6 inches above the ground, measured at the heel.

The Mid-Step March Feet are raised 6 to 12 inches above the ground.

The High-Step March Feet are raised 12 to 24 inches from the ground, approximately knee high to waist high.

Knee Ups With each march step pull knees up to chest.

The Walk Kick Step This is a walker's version of the jump kick. Without jumping, you raise your straight leg as you walk forward, using the opposite straight arm swing to counterbalance your leg movements. The kick step is a straight-legged step with no knee bending, or at most only slight knee bending.

Walk kick steps can be practiced both in-place and on the move.

Low Kick Step Lift each leg 3 to 6 inches off the ground. Bend your knee only slightly during the step. If you're stepping in place, put your foot back down in the same place you started from. If you are stepping on the move, place your foot down 12 to 24 inches in front of you. Be sure your toes are pointed in the direction of travel. Practice each kick step for 6 to 12 counts.

Mid Kick Step Lift each leg 12 to 24 inches off the ground.

High Kick Step Lift each leg 24 to 48 inches off the ground.

Leg Extensions (with Ankle Weights)

Bend and raise your leg knee high. Extend the leg slowly back to the straightened position and hold for two counts. Bend it just as slowly back again. Place foot back on the ground—in-place walkers place the foot in the same spot, on-the-move walkers place it 6-12 inches in front. Repeat the leg extension exercise with the other foot. Repeat each leg 6-12 counts.

Back Leg Extension (In place only) Bend leg back and hold for two counts. Slowly straighten leg as you place it back down in its original position. Repeat Back Leg Extension on the other foot. Repeat each leg 6-12 counts.

Crossover Steps (In place only) Step over the opposite foot, placing moving foot parallel to the supporting foot, but do not make contact with the ground. Instead, return foot to its original position. Repeat on each leg 12-20 counts.

Back and Abdomen

The Hoe Down The Hoe Down exercise involves walking while bending at the waist. Cotton planters known as "hoe downers" would walk along the plowed furrows, a short hoe in one hand, a plant seedling in the other. In a synchronized arm and waist bending motion, the hoe would come down digging a hole, and the seedling would be dropped in. The hoe downer would then use his arm in an overhead swinging motion to cover dirt over the roots of the plant.

The walking exercise version of the Hoe Down involves arm pumping and waist bending. Bend forward during the first two steps and bend backward during the next two steps. Or, alternately bend forward one step and backward the next step, all the time pumping with the arms. Beginners should bend at 45-degree angles (¼ Hoe Down), advanced walkers can bend to 90 degrees (½ Hoe Down), which is almost parallel with the ground. Practice the Hoe Down for 6 to 12 counts.

This exercise feels awkward at first, but you will get used to it with practice.

Variations: Try the Hoe Down with high and low pumping arms. Use double arm pumps with the Hoe Down to simulate the movements of a cross-country skier who is double poling.

The Stork Step This is a variation of the march step that allows you to lift your legs higher while still moving forward. As you lift your leg forward, raise your knee to your chest. (Bend at the waist as you bring your knees to your chest.) Then, like a stork, swing it out gradually in an arc motion. Lead with your toes in an up and down arc and use the forefoot strike to make contact with the ground. The more experienced you become at stork walking, the higher and smoother your toe arcs will become. The Stork Walk is a good abdominal exercise.

The Camel Walk The camel walk is a walk with a kneebend. After completing the heel strike, bend your leg instead of straightening it and sink down on the supporting leg as you lift the swing leg up. You will be using the camel walk during various waist bending exercises to take pressure off your lower back when bending. Practice the Camel Walk on each leg for 6 to 12 counts.

The Hip Walk On the move: When walking while weight loaded, strive to extend your hip forward with each leg extension and to control your leg action throughout the whole walking cycle. Do not let your foot, loaded with ankle weights, merely dangle; work it through the leg swing phase.

In place: Hip walk in place by raising your hip as you lift your leg. Repeat hip walk on each leg for 6 to 12 counts.

Bent Leg Hip Step Bend your leg as you would normally and follow the leg lift through with an extension upward of the hip on the same side. Repeat on each leg for 6 to 12 counts.

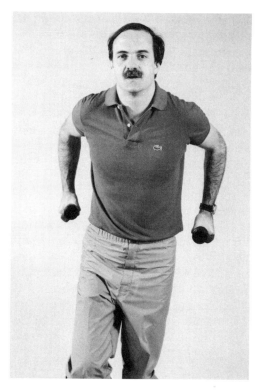

Straight Leg Hip Step Do not bend your leg when you lift it. Instead, raise the whole leg with your hip. This leg action will emphasize your hip step even more. Repeat straight leg hip walk on each leg for 6 to 12 counts.

Side Bends with Weights Bend from side to side while you rotate slightly forward. Lift the leg opposite the bending side and cross it over to that side.

A Note on Combining Weightwalk Calisthenic Exercises

Until now you have practiced the individual arm, leg, and waist movements as separate exercises. After you have done this for six weeks or more, you can combine certain arm and leg movements as calisthenic routines. For example, you can do the Hoe Down with high leg lifts. The lateral arm raises can be done while walking or march stepping in place.

Here are some general rules to follow about combination exercises:

1. If your upper body is working harder than your lower body, you should work your lower body less strenuously. For example, a high arm pump should be matched with a low step. Once you have reached a high degree of muscular and aerobic fitness, you can increase the workloads at all levels, but this will come only after many months of training.

2. Generally speaking, your arm, leg, and trunk arcs for upper, lower, and middle areas of your body should be synchronized. A full arm arc should be accompanied by a full leg arc or higher leg lift.

3. The greater the weight you add to your arms and legs, the slower your pace and the shorter your range of movement. Do not increase speed and weight loading too fast. Gauge yourself. Wait until you are fit enough to take on the increased weight.

Now that you have been introduced to the new steps and movements you will need for your Weightwalk Workout you are almost ready to begin. There are just a few more things you need to know:

How to Determine the Weight Load*

You should use heavier weights during the techniques routine than during the aerobic routine. To determine the amount of weight, find out what your maximum weight capacity is for one single movement and train at 25-50% of that weight. So, if the heaviest weight your bicep can curl is 50 pounds, then 12-25 pounds should be your weight loading range.

Aerobic Weight Loading

For aerobic weight loading you should train with no more than half the calisthenics load for each limb (1 to 10 pounds), and up to a maximum of 40 pounds for trunk or backpack weight. Before you carry any weight, your muscles must first be trained. By practicing your walking techniques and calisthenics weight loaded, you will be able to strengthen different body parts for the Weightwalk aerobics.

Repetitions

Repetitions or "reps" is a weight and calisthenic training term for the number of complete movements up and down, back and forth, or out and in of an exercise of a specific group of muscles, like those of your right arm and shoulder. A walking repetition involves a complete walking cycle or individual steps, arm swings, arm

*See Table 15, p. 102.

pumps, waist bends. Every time you take a few steps walking you are doing a series of arm leg repetitions similar to what calisthenics practitioners and body builders do. As you become more fit, repeat the Weightwalk techniques and calisthenics routines two to three times. Each time is referred to as a "set" of exercises or repetitions.

How to Pick Up Weights

Whenever picking up hand-held or other weights from the ground, be sure to bend your knees. Keep your upper body as erect as possible when reaching down for the weight, and use your leg muscles to raise the weight. Avoid lifting with your lower back.

TABLE 16: WEIGHTWALK CALISTHENICS

Level	Sets	Arm or Leg Repetitions	Torso Repetitions
I	1x	8-10	8-10
II	1x	10-12	10-13
III	2x	12-20	12-20 (over 50 years of age) 20-30 (under 50 years of age)
IV	3x	20-30	20-30 (over 50 years of age) 30-50 (under 50 years of age)
V	4x	30-50	30 and up (over 50 years of age) 50 and up (under 50 years of age)

The Weightwalk Workout

Weightwalk Warm-up

(2 to 5 minutes)

Start your Weightwalk Warm-up with a slow, 60 steps-per-minute pace and build to as high as 100 steps per minute. During the course of your warm-up, increase both the range of arm and leg motion and the rapidity of the arm and leg movements. Stay in the 60 to 100 steps per minute range.

In Place

Practice gradually lifting your legs higher from the low march step (3 to 6 inches from the ground) to the mid-step march (6 to 12 inches from the ground) and up to the knee ups. Do each step for 30 to 60 seconds. At the same time, pump your arms in ever increasing arcs.

Vary this routine by marching two to four steps forward and back. You can also practice marching with crossover steps (see p. 131). Be sure each step you take has the proper leg lift. Begin to incorporate the special Weightwalk Steps and arm movement techniques you have learned (the Stork and Camel Walks, for example) into your March Step Series. Also practice the standard Weightwalk arm pumping series during your warm-up walk.

On the Move

You can do your Weightwalk warm-up on the move using march steps while moving forward, or you can step out with longer strides and higher arm pumps. Weightwalkers on the move should start with straight arm pumps, gradually increasing the length and height of the swings. During the straight arm pumps your step rate should be 60 steps per minute. As you change to bent arm pumps your step rate should increase to 90 to 120 steps per minute. Vary your arm pumps with double arm, overhead, crossover and cradle swing.

Weightwalk Warm-Up Stretching

(5 to 10 minutes)

The lower back stretch is perhaps the single most important preparation for the Weightwalk Workout. The body has a tendency to transfer the weight load to the back because it is closest to the center of gravity. The squat stretch (see p. 50) and the spinal twist (see p. 61) are also important stretching exercises to practice both before and after walking with weights.

For the warm-up stretches, do the Basic Four Walker's Stretches and then go to the special Weightwalk stretches.

The Basic Four

1. The Calf and Achilles Tendon Stretch (p. 35)

2. The Quadriceps and Ankle Stretch (p. 36)

3. The Hamstring Stretch (p. 37)

4. The Flying Lunge Stretch (p. 39)

   For Specific Body Areas
   Triceps and Shoulder Stretch (p. 44)
   Upper Back Stretch (p. 49)
   Chest and Shoulder Stretch (p. 45)
   Standing Back and Hip Stretch (p. 51)
   Knee Ups (p. 52)
   Squat Stretch (p. 50)
   Lower Back Stretch (p. 50)

Weightwalk Techniques and Calisthenics

(5 to 10 minutes)

The following series of exercises will train your whole body by using isolated walking movements. Start with your upper body, then go to your middle body, and finish with your legs. After completing the first six-week training period, continue to practice these exercises as weight training movements, repeating them in two or three sets as you increase the weight load according to the schedule in Table 15 (p. 102). Beginners and those who have never handled barbell weights should practice the walking movements without weights for the first two weeks. (Unless otherwise indicated, beginners should do each exercise 12 counts, advanced 20 counts.)

Weightwalk Calisthenics

Arm Pumping Series

Straight Arm Pumps (Short Swings)
Back and Forth Straight Arm Pumps
1. Waist high

2. Chest high

3. Shoulder high

4. Overhead

Crossover Pumps
1. Straight arm chest to shoulder high

2. Bent arms crossover pumps chest high

3. Overhead cradle

Bent Arm Pumps and Curls
1. Single Arms: Back and Forth
   90-degree pump and curl
   45-degree pump (uppercuts)
   a. chest high uppercuts
   b. overhead uppercuts

Double Arm Pumps Back and Forth
1. Shoulder high (90 degrees)

2. Overhead (45 degrees)

Triceps Extension
1. Parallel Double Straight Arm Pumps
   a. Slightly bending waist
   b. Bending waist at 90 degrees

Straight Arm Raises
1. Side raises

2. Front raises

Shoulder Shrugs Weight Loaded
Double Arm Presses
1. Chest presses

2. Front shoulder press

3. Back shoulder press

Cradle Arm Pumps
1. Overhead Cradle

2. Side Cradle

Bicep Curls
1. From sides

2. From elbows shoulder high

Bent Arm Flyes
1. Breast Beaters

2. Elbow Flyes

Weightwalk Aerobics

(15 to 30 minutes)

In the following four aerobic Weightwalk segments, the exercises you have practiced during the Techniques and Calisthenics portion of your Workout are combined. Now you will be using lighter weights and a higher number of repetitions. (See Table 15, p. 102.)

Routine #1: The Wind-Up (1 minute) This will help you achieve a wide range of arm and leg movements while walking with hand-held and ankle weights. You should reach the aerobic heart training zone during this period. If you don't, pick up the pace to 90 to 120 steps per minute or add a weight belt or a weight loaded backpack.

Cadence: Beginners 45 to 60 arm/leg repetitions per minute; advanced 60 to 90.

Practice straight arm, slow, and full arc swings with accompanying slow, full march steps. Concentrate on a full range of movement. Go from a ¼ arc to a full arc using 60 repetitions for each arc.

Special Note: Beginners can use the standard Pacewalk Workout warm-up without weights. Advanced walkers should use one pound weights in hand and one pound weights on each ankle for this portion of the Workout.

Starting Position: Use a wider stance for the Weightwalk Workout. In place, feet should be shoulder–width apart; on the move, 3 to 5 inches apart.

Arms	Time in Seconds	Legs	Cadence
Straight Arms:		*March Step:*	*SPM:*
¼ arc	60	¼ step	90
½ arc	60	½ step	90
Full arc	60	Full step	60
¼ arc	40	¼ step	60
Overhead			
Swing ¼ arc	60	knee ups	30

or:

Practice Weightwalk on the move (5 minutes) at a moderate pace with wide strides and high arm pumps (full-120 arc arm swing). Pump with your arms, not your shoulders. Practice walking techniques (for example, holding proper posture, heel strike, outer edge roll, straightening the supporting leg, toe-off). Pump arms straight back and forth.

Routine #2: Training Body Parts (10-15 minutes)

Cadence: Beginner's steady pace for aerobic training zone. Estimate 60 steps per minute (this will vary depending on fitness level). Advanced estimate 90 steps per minute.

Weight Load: See Table 15.

Starting Position: Continue walking with the Weightwalker's wide stance.

Upper Body Work	Seconds/Counts	Accompanying Weightwalk Steps	Pace (SPM)
Bent Arms Pump:			
90-degree	60	½ march	90-100
45-degree	60	¼ march	100-120
Overhead Pumps	60	¼ march	100-120
Bent Arms Pump:			
Double Arm Pump (Shoulder High)	15	½ march	90-100
Double Arm Pump (Overhead)	15	¼ march	90-100
Cradle Arm Pumps (Overhead)	15	¼ march	90-100
Crossover Pumps			
Waist High	60	¼ march	100-120
Chest High	60	½ march	100-120
Cradle Pumps			
Left	30	¼ march	90-100
Right	30	¼ march	90-100
Arm Presses			
From Chest	15	½ march	90-100
From Shoulders	15	½ march	90-100
From Back	15	½ march	90-100
Flyes			
Straight Arm	15	½ march	90-100
Bent Arm	15	½ march	90-100
Elbow Arm	15	½ march	90-100
Bicep Curls	15	½ march	90-100
Tricep Extensions			
Bent Over ¼ (45 degrees)	15	¼ march	90-100
Bent Over ½ (90 degrees)	15	¼ march	90-100
Straight Arm Presses			
Front	15	½-full march	90-100
Side	15	½-full march	90-100
Shoulder Shrugs	15	½-full march	60-90

Middle Body Work	Seconds/ Counts	Accompanying Weightwalk Steps	Pace (SPM)
Hoe Downs (90-degree bent arm)			
¼ Bend (45 degrees)	15-30	½-full march	60-90
½ Bend (90 degrees)	15-30	½-full march	60-90
Hip Walks (45-degree bent arm)			
(In Place)			
Bent Leg	30-60	¼ march	60-90
Straight Leg	30-60	¼ march	60-90
On the Move (Straight arm pump 90-degree bent arm)			
Hip Extension	60		60-90
Side Bends (In place)	30	¼ march	60-90
Cradle			
Left	30	¼ march	90-100
Right	30	¼ march	90-100

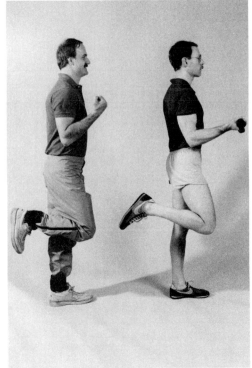

Lower Body Work	Seconds/ Counts	Arm Work	Pace (SPM)
Leg Extension (In Place)			
Left-Right	15	Overhead Pumps	45-60
Kick Steps	60	Straight Arm Swings	45-60
Back Step/Lifts (In Place)	15	Same Arm 90 Degree Bent Arm Pumps	
Crossover Steps			
Right Step - 3	15	Cradle-Right	45-60
Left Step - 3	15	Cradle-Left	45-60
Camel Walk	60	45-degree arm	45-60
Stork Walk	60	90-degree arm	45-60

Routine #3: Fast Steady Pace (10 minutes) Maintain a fast, steady aerobic training pace using hand-held, leg and trunk loaded weights while executing simple arm and step movements.

Cadence: Beginners 90 to 120 steps per minute; advanced 120-140 steps per minute.

Weight Load: See Table 15: Weight Loading Schedule on page 102.
Starting Position: In place: narrow stance, feet 3 to 5 inches apart. On the move: feet 3 to 5 inches apart.

Legs	Accompanying Arms
In Place	
March Step Series (3-5 sets)	Use arm swings that correspond with the leg arcs
On the Move	
Pacewalk Routine while fully weight loaded	Straight Arm Pumps, Bent Arm Pumps

The Weightwalk Cool-Down

(2-5 minutes)

Slow Down Walk

Slow down your walking pace to 60 to 90 spm in one minute intervals, as you did in the Pacewalk Cool-Down. Put down hand-held and ankle weights and do your walking free of any weight.

Light Stretching and Relaxing

Stretch areas worked the most.

Cool-Down Stretches

1. Squat stretch (see p. 50)
2. Spinal Twist (see p. 61)
3. Seated Groin Stretch (see p. 60)
4. Lying Down Neck Stretch (see p. 63)
5. Overhead Leg Stretch (see p. 62)

The Climbwalk Workout

T o THOSE OF YOU who suffer from the pain and injury of overtraining with other high intensity workouts, I dedicate the Climbwalk Workout. It will give you great exercise benefits without great pains. The Climbwalk Workout combines two types of resistance (gravity and friction) with a wide range of speeds.

The Climbwalk is probably the most vigorous of the four Walking Workouts. Climbwalks burn between 500 and 1500 calories in an hour, depending on your speed and body weight. Also, you can combine Climbing with Pacewalking and Weightwalking for the highest intensity Workout possible.

The Climbwalk consists of two Workouts, hill climbing and step climbing. Stairs are good for slower paced workouts because you must work harder against gravity on each step. Since stair steps are usually less than one foot apart, you have to shorten your stride length and concentrate on lifting your legs higher instead of swinging them further forward. Since a wider stride contributes more to your overall walking speed than to moving your legs faster, it is difficult to step climb at a speed higher than 120 steps per minute (four miles per hour). Of course, you can skip steps (take two at a time) and get a wider stride as well as a higher leg lift. I recommend skipping steps to increase your walking speed, using the stride-stretch approach.

You can Pacewalk with proper training at 5.5 miles per hour (150 spm) on a smooth sloped surface, but it is unlikely that you could keep up this pace on a rough slope. Once the slope angle approaches that of a staircase, it is harder to walk with a long stride.

The Muscles Worked

Climbing, more than other forms of walking, works the stomach, buttocks, and lower back. In fact, climbing actually works *all* your muscles more than any other form of walking, because with each step you walk *twice:* once forward and once up. When you walk up you use your leg and waist muscles to lift your whole body. Not only do you support the weight of your body on one leg, but you also use that leg to lift up your body. The best analogy would be a deep knee bend or squat in weight training, except that in climbing you don't strain your knees and lower back as much. A step climber lifts his own body weight, which is better distributed than barbell weights could ever be.

It is possible to experience some back strain from the Climbwalk exercises if you overdo them, but it is more likely that you will feel the effects of stair work in your gluteus maximus (buttocks). Stretch the hips, legs, and lower back before and after the exercises.

Technique #13

The Forefoot Strike-Heel Press Down

When stair climbing you use the forefoot strike (ball of your foot) first, then you press the heel down and straighten the supporting leg. This action stretches your calf muscles, keeping them from becoming overstrained during the Workout. If you do not complete the heel strike in this manner, you'll be walking on your forefoot. Too much of this kind of walking will shorten your calf muscles and they will hurt after every Workout.

When slope climbing, it is important to continue as long as possible to strike with your *heel* first. When the angle of ascent makes it too difficult to do this, switch to the forefoot strike. As you would on stairs, press your heel firmly down after making contact, and straighten the supporting leg.

Practice the forefoot strike and heel press down on stairs or on a steep incline for 12 to 20 counts.

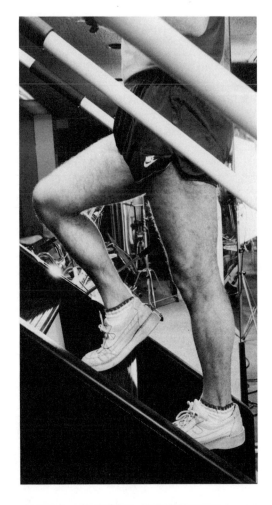

The Modified Heel Strike

Technique #14

The surface of many stairs is not deep enough for you to place your whole foot down, so you need to adopt a modified heel strike. Land on your forefoot or mid-foot and then press down your foot, letting the heel hang off the edge of the step.

Since you can't feel your heel striking anything, you should focus instead on straightening the leg and bending the knee back slightly.

Practice the Modified Heel Strike on each foot for 6 to 12 counts.

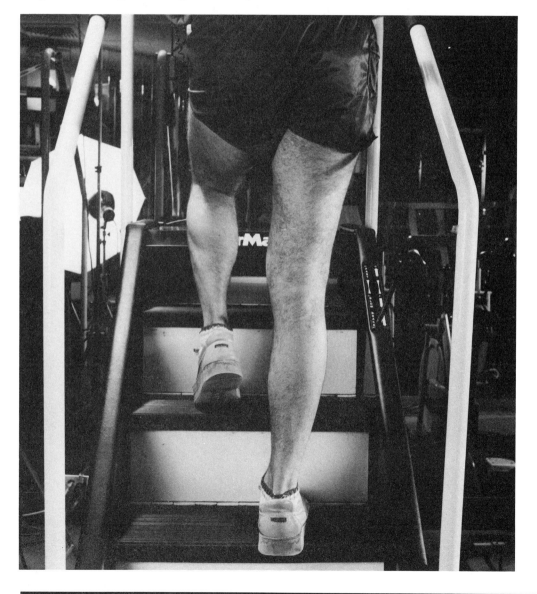

Technique #15

Crossover Step-Ups

Do your crossover step-ups on stairs or on a slope in the same way as on a flat surface.

Practice crossover step-ups on each leg for 6 to 12 counts.

Side Step-Ups

Technique #16

With your body turned sideways, step up with the leading foot and bring the other foot up parallel to it. On the way down, reverse the motion. Side stepping is often the only safe way to descend on rugged terrain. It is also the only effective way to walk up and down slopes on skis.

Both the side step-ups and crossover step-ups work the outer and inner thigh muscles. The training effect can be enhanced through the use of ankle weights (see Table 15, p. 102).

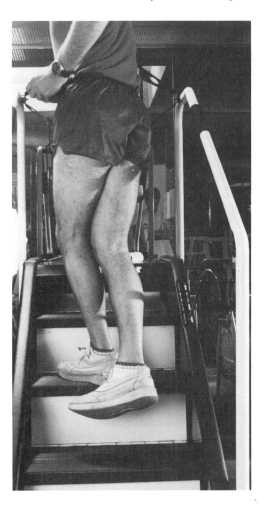

Technique #17

Back Step-Ups

This is basically climbing stairs backwards. Do back step-ups as you would back step on a flat surface, leading and striking with your forefoot first, and then rolling back to your heel. It is important to press down the heel and straighten the supporting leg. You'll find this easier to do than on the front step-up because you'll be using your heel rather than your toe to push off.

Practice back stepping up for 6 to 12 counts.

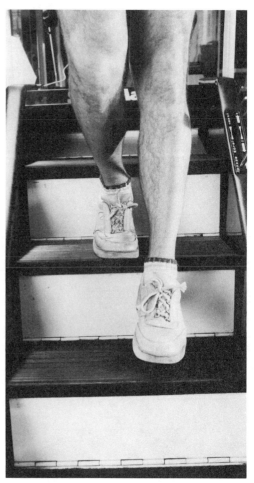

TABLE 17: STEP CLIMBING AND INCREASING FLOORS
Floors and Climbing Speed by Fitness Levels per Session

Week	I		II		III		IV		V	
	FLRS	SPM	FLRS	SPM	FLRS	SPM	FLRS	SPM	FLRS	SPM
1	5	30	15	40	40	60	85	100	130	130
2	7	30	20	50	45	75	90	105	140	140
3	9	30	25	50	55	80	100	110	150	145
4	11	40	30	55	65	90	110	110	160	150
5	13	40	35	55	75	90	120	120	180	155
6	15	40	40	60	85	100	130	120	200	160

Notes on Step Climbing
Buildings. Floors and stairways contain long (24 steps) and short (13 steps) flights.

Residential. Apartment buildings have 2-4 flights with about 16 steps for each floor. Private homes generally have one flight per floor of 13-15 steps per flight. Angles of ascent vary.

Flights into Miles. You can measure your stair and hill climbing into miles walk climbed. They're worth 2-5 times the caloric expenditure of flat miles depending on the slope grade walked. Depending on riser height and step number there are 2,600 stair steps to the mile or approximately 160-200 flights per mile (13-16 steps per flight).

Slope. The angle of ascent for most stairs ranges from 20-30 degrees. If you use the same stairways repeatedly you can measure the angle of ascent by using a protractor or other angle-measuring device and measure the angle of tilt of the bottom side of the stairway where it meets the ground or by drawing an imaginary line between the edges of two consecutive risers and measuring the angle of that line using the steps' platform as your base. Then use the caloric tables for incline walking to get the caloric value of your climb.

Basic Rule: Try to walk down a stairway as many times as you walked up because it will balance muscle development in the front and back of the legs.

Combinations: You can combine stair or hill work with other exercise routines or use it as a substitute for speed work. Climbing stairs is generally slow walking so you can combine it with weight loaded walking and move at 1-2 mph slower than with fast walking weight loaded routines.

TABLE 18: CALORIC EXPENDITURE AT VARIOUS SPEEDS AND GRADES FOR HILL AND SLOPE WALKING

Grade		Speed(mph)				
		LEVEL				
		I	**II**	**III**	**IV**	**V**
Percent	**Degrees**	**1.5**	**2.25**	**3.00**	**3.75**	**4.50**
40	21.8	12.1				
35	19.3	11.2				
30	16.7	9.7	18.1			
25	14.0	8.3	15.1			
20	11.3	7.1	12.4	12.9		
15	8.5	5.9	10.1	10.5	14.5	
10	5.7	4.9	8.2	8.5	12.0	15.1
5	2.9	4.2	6.5	6.7	11.0	13.1
0	0	2.9	4.3	5.7	7.1	8.6
− 5	− 2.9	2.3	3.3	4.4	5.3	6.4
− 10	− 5.7	2.2	3.0	3.9	4.7	5.5
− 15	− 8.5	2.4	3.2	4.0	4.7	5.4
− 20	− 11.3	3.0	4.0	4.8	5.5	6.0
− 25	− 14.0	3.3	4.6	5.7	6.5	6.8
− 30	− 16.7	3.4	4.9	6.1	6.8	7.0
− 35	− 19.3	3.5	5.2	6.6	7.2	7.2
− 40	− 21.8	4.0	6.1	7.8	8.4	8.2

Energy expenditure is measured in calories per minute (cpm) for a subject weighing 157 pounds. Note how cpm goes down then gradually increases again as downhill grade grows steeper. This is due to the need for braking against the momentum of going down too fast.

TABLE 19: CLIMBWALK MET LEVELS
Stair climbing speed:

mph	spm	METS	Exercise Calories per Hour	For Fitness Level	mph	spm	METS	Exercise Calories per Hour	For Fitness Level
1	30	5	300	I	3.7	105	13	1000	IV
1.5	40	6	400	II	3.75	110	14	1050	
2.25	55	7	440		4.0	120	15	1100	
2.5	60	8	550						
					4.5	130	16	1200	V
2.75	75	9	650	III	4.75	135	17	1285	
2.85	80	10	750		5	140	18	1340	
3	90	11	850		5.25	145	19	1400	
3.5	100	12	950		5.5	150	20	1480	
					5.75	155	21	1560	
					6	160	22	1630	

The Climbwalk Workout

The Warm-up Climbwalk

(2 to 5 minutes)

Slow Climbing

You can use any of the Pacewalk or Weightwalk warm-ups, or you can start with a slow stair or hill climb (45 to 60 steps per minute). When stepping forward up stairs or walking up an incline, be sure to keep your toes pointed in the direction of travel. Pump your opposite arm with each climbing step. During your warm-up climb, execute a series of slow wide-range arm movements like the overhead cradle, high straight arm swings, windmill, or just light arm pumping to warm up your upper body. If you are in excellent shape, you can warm up with a faster paced climb (90 to 120 steps per minute).

Climbwalk Warm-Up Stretching

Concentrate on stretching the lower back and the backs of your legs. Do the following stretches:

The Basic Four

1. The Calf and Achilles Tendon Stretch (p. 35)

2. The Quadriceps and Ankle Stretch (p. 36)

3. The Hamstring Stretch (p. 37)

4. The Flying Lunge Stretch (p. 39)

   Specifically for the Climbwalk Workout
   Squat Stretch (p. 50)
   Hang Over Stretch (p. 56)

Climbwalk Techniques and Calisthenics

After you have learned the basic climbing steps, practice them in combination with the following arm pumping movements during the techniques and calisthenics portion of your Workout.*

 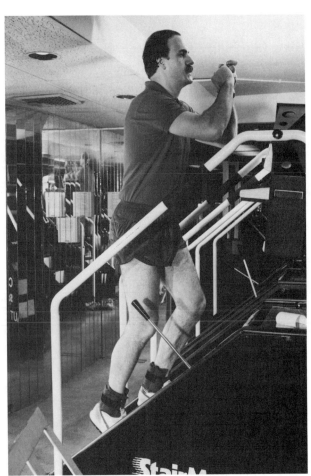

With the Forward Step-Ups and Back Step-Ups Practice:
Bent Arm Pumps: Shoulder High (p. 77)
Overhead Pump (p. 78)
Overhead Cradle (p. 120)

*Warning: Always be extra careful when climbing stairs or a slope. Be sure you have a surface which provides you with good footing. Do not take risks which would lead you to lose your balance and fall.

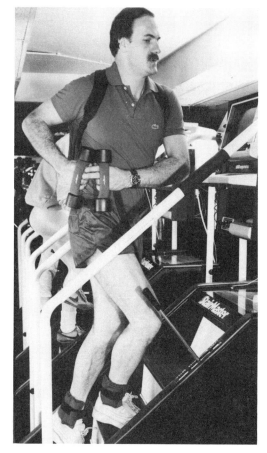

With the Crossover Step-Ups and Side Step-Ups Practice:
Cradle Pumps and the Overhead Cradle

With the Back Step-Ups Practice:
Side Cradle and 90-degree Arm Pumps

Climbwalk Aerobics

(15-30 minutes)

The METS Table (p. 103) shows you the work load for different climbing speeds. Start your Climbwalk Workout aerobics by setting your goals for speed (steps per minute) and distances on a slope. Determine these according to your present fitness level.

The Climbwalk Cool-Down

(2-5 minutes)

Reduce your pace in one-minute intervals as you did in the Pacewalk and Weightwalk cool-downs. Practice: the squat stretch (p. 50), the Groin and Lower Back Stretch (p. 60), Elevating Feet (p. 63), and the Hang Over Stretch (p. 56).

4 The Dancewalk Workout

START THE MUSIC! Now the real fun begins. If you are already an aerobic dancer or do aerobic calisthenics, you know how music can spice up an exercise session. The Dancewalk gives you an opportunity to be creative, exercise indoors in front of the stereo, and combine all the techniques from the other Walking Workouts.

The Dancewalk Workout combines all the walking movements you have learned so far in a continuous exercise. This dance-style Workout for both men and women can be practiced in a relatively small place,

without special equipment, in less than one hour. A special weight training segment is included, but advanced walkers may want to use arm and leg weights throughout most of the Workout.

Before you begin the Dancewalk Workout have ready whatever equipment and attachments you are presently using for your Pacewalk, Weightwalk, and Climbwalk Workouts (step-up bench, hand and ankle weights, for example) because we will be integrating portions of these Workout routines into the aerobic conditioning segment of the Dancewalk.

The Dancewalk Workout

The Dancewalk Warm-Up

If you walk for at least 10 minutes prior to the Workout, you will have already completed the warm-up phase, and you can go on to stretching. Throughout the Dancewalk Workout, remember to practice holding proper posture and to synchronize arm/leg swinging with breathing. Use a six-count cadence with appropriate accompanying music.

Warm-Up Breathing and Posture

Stand in the Basic Starting Position, feet hip-distance apart, toes pointed in the direction of travel, arms hanging relaxed at your sides. Align your head, chest, shoulders, and abdomen over your hips and pelvis. Practice stomach and buttocks tucking. Breathe easily, exhaling and inhaling to the beat of the music, six counts. Now, belly breathe six counts.

Walking in Place

Walk in place swinging your arms in increasingly longer arcs. Remember to let your arms swing in a natural arc from front to back, back to front.

Straight Arm Swing and Walk

Low Pumps-Waist High   6 counts   Medium Pumps-Chest High   6 counts

Overhead Pumps   6 counts
Windmill-Full Swing   6 counts

Marching in Place

March in place using leg lifts ranging from 12 inches off the ground to knee at chest level. Your arms should swing (and pump) with the same rhythm and arc as your legs. Use bent and low arm swings and pumps.

Marching In Place Accompanied by Arm Swings

Legs		*Arms*
Leg lifts 12″	6 counts	90-degree Bent Arms
¼ March Step (16″-18″)	6 counts	90-degree Bent Arms
½ March Step (24″)	6 counts	45-degree Uppercuts
Full March Step	6 counts	45-degree Bent Arm Pumps

Dancewalk Stretching

(2-5 minutes)

After walking or marching in place, your muscles should be warmed up enough to begin stretching. Be careful to stretch slowly and don't let the music cause you to bounce. Remember, the music for this portion should be slow.

The Basic Four Stretches (Hold 15-20 counts each)

1. The Calf and Achilles Tendon Stretch (p. 35)

2. The Quadriceps and Ankle Stretch (p. 36)

3. The Hamstring Stretch (p. 37)

4. The Flying Lunge Stretch (p. 39)

Hip Stretches
Beginners: Standing Hip Stretch (see p. 53)
Advanced: Raised Leg Hip Stretch (see p. 54)

Light Stretching Warm-Up Routines

Head Rolls Standing or walking in place in the Basic Starting Position, feet hip-distance apart, toes pointed in the direction of travel, roll your neck clockwise once, then counterclockwise once. Bend your head forward once, and back once. Repeat 3 times.

Shoulder Shrugs and Windmills Shrug your shoulders up to your ears and rotate them down, back, and up again for 6 to 8 counts. Repeat, reversing the direction for 6 to 8 counts. Be sure to maintain good posture, stomach and abdomen tucked in. Breathe normally.

Reach Ups While walking in place, reach up over your head with both arms. Repeat for 8 to 16 counts.

Side Bends Bend to the side while slightly lifting up the hip and leg on that side to help walking in place. Do the same on the other side. Repeat for 6 to 8 counts.

The Cradle Clasp hands in front and swing arms from side to side, reaching back as far as you can. Also look back as you swing. Repeat for 6 to 8 counts on each side.

Hoe Downs Bend slowly at the waist, (beginners 45 degrees; advanced 90 degrees). Keeping knees bent, keeping yourself bent over, walk while you pump your arms overhead. Repeat for 6 to 8 counts.

Heel Walk Walk on heels then on toes, each for 12 to 20 counts.

Heel-Toe Rock Rock from your heels to your toes and back for 6 to 8 counts.

Stride Stretches From the Basic Starting Position, lift and swing one leg forward, landing on your heel. Hold this position, checking that you have proper posture. Now, lift the leg and place it an additional four inches (beginner) or eight inches (advanced) forward. Feel your stride stretching and your hip leaning into the stride. Repeat with each leg for 3 to 4 counts.

Dancewalk Techniques and Calisthenics

(5 to 10 minutes)

Practice these body training routines with or without weights, depending on your level of muscular conditioning. In this portion of the Dancewalk you can play music with a fast tempo. According to your level of fitness, you will either have to walk in place or march with knees up.

Part One: The Windup

The Robot The Robot is slow motion walking. Practice each of the stages of the walking cycle in slow motion, concentrating on proper position and execution. Ideally you should watch yourself in a full-length mirror. If that's not possible, watch your different body parts as you execute the movements.

The Robot #1: The One Step Take one step forward in slow motion, carefully executing walking techniques #1-12.

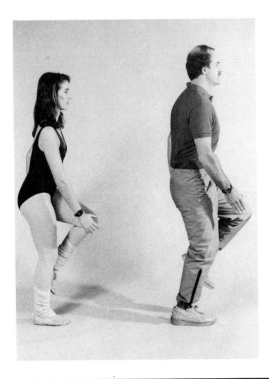

The Robot #2: The Two Step Take two steps forward in slow motion, carefully executing walking techniques #1-12. Return to Starting Position, back stepping two steps in slow motion.

The Robot #3: The Three Step Moving in slow motion:

  3 steps forward
  3 steps back
  3 crossover steps left with 3 cradle arm swings left
  3 crossover steps right with 3 cradle arm swings right

Repeat 3 steps left and right for 6 to 8 counts.

Note: Be sure each leg repetition is accompanied by an opposite arm repetition. Concentrate on holding your posture and pulling your leg under your body. Be sure your toes are pointed upward 45 degrees at the heel strike and that they are pointed in the direction of travel (except during crossovers and side steps, of course). Roll on the outer edge of your foot.

Shuffle Step with Straight Arm Pumps (4 sets, 6 counts each) Pace 60 to 90 steps per minute. Swing arms higher and higher with each set.

Set 1: Straight arm pumps, chest high, ¼ walk kick step
Set 2: Straight arm pumps, head high, ½ walk kick step
Set 3: Windmill—Single arms, ¾ walk kick step
Set 4: Windmill—Double arms

Part Two: Training Body Parts

Now, work shifts to the upper body as you start the "training your body parts" section of the Dancewalk. Beginners should walk during this portion; advanced exercisers can march in place.

Uppers (Upper back, shoulders, chest, arms) With or without hand and ankle weights, make a fist or hold a hand weight with each of the following exercises.

Shoulders 1 (deltoids, trapezius) Straight arm shoulder rotations. Rotate straight arms at shoulder height for 6 to 8 counts each.

Shoulders 2 (deltoids) Flappers: Raise and lower arms for 6 to 8 counts.

Shoulders 3 (deltoids, trapezius) Presses: Bend elbows, hands at shoulder height. Straighten arms. Push arms up over head from chest, from shoulder, and from back of shoulder for 20 to 30 counts.

Shoulder 4: (deltoids, trapezius) Windmill: Double arm swing overhead for 12 to 20 counts.

Arms 1 (Biceps) Bicep curl: At chest level, raise and lower forearms for 20 to 30 counts. Repeat bicep curls from shoulder level as chest and upper back exercise.

Arms 2 (Triceps) Tricep Flyes: Extend arms at shoulder level, palms down, bend arms at 90 degrees and extend out again. Repeat for 15 to 20 counts.

Chest 1 Pectoral Flyes: With hands at shoulder level, bring elbows together in front of chest.

Chest 2 Uppercuts: With hands at waist level, swing arms alternately with opposite leg swings. Swing arms across chest to opposite shoulder. Repeat #1 and #2 for 20 to 30 counts.

Chest 3 Crossover Swings with straight arm.

Middles (abdominals, hips, buttocks, obliques, lower back)

Hip 1 Hip Walking: Bend from side to side as you lift the leg on the same side. Do this exercise with either straight or bent knees. Repeat for 20 to 30 counts.

Hip 2 Straight Leg Kick Walks: March in place with straight leg lifts opposite straight arm swings. Repeat each leg for 20 to 30 counts.

Hip 3 Knee Ups: Lift knees to chest with opposite bent arm swings. Keep head erect and back straight. Repeat each knee up for 12 to 20 counts.

Abdominal 1 Hoe Downs: Beginners bend down one quarter of the way to floor. Hold two counts, then straighten up slowly. Advanced exercisers should bend half way to floor. Bend so that your upper body is parallel to the ground. Swing arms and legs, bent or straight out, while walking or marching in place. Repeat for 10 to 20 counts. With the Hoe Down you can vary the types of leg and arm swings for a greater training effect. Use straight leg kick walks, knee-ups, back step kicks. Use straight arm swings, biceps curls, tricep flyes.

March Steps in Place with Bent Arm Pumps
(3 sets, 6 counts each)
    Count out loud and pick up pace (90 to 120 spm)

Arm Swings/March Steps

    Set 1: Bent arm swings, chest high (90 degrees)
    ¼ (12 to 18 inches high) leg lifts
    Set 2: Bent arm swings, chest high (90 degrees)
    ½ (18 to 24 inches-waist high) knee ups
    Set 3: Uppercuts (45 degrees)

Note: Concentrate on lifting your legs high, beginners' knees should be waist high; advanced, knees to the chest. Opposite arms should be pumping, beginners, chest high; advanced, uppercuts. If you have difficulty keeping the pace with marching steps, alternate with walk kick steps half as high as the knee of your supporting leg. Repeat: Beginners, 90 counts per minute; advanced, 120 counts per minute.

Legs 1 Back Step Kicks: With weight slightly forward, kick leg out behind body. Opposite arm should swing back as opposite leg is kicking back.

    Repeat the above series of calisthenics with the three steps front, back, and crossover step movement where appropriate:

    Three Steps Forward and back
    Shoulders 1, 2, 3
    Bicep Curl
    Tricep Flyes
    Crossover Arm Swings 1, 2
    Hip Walking (hip extension)
    Straight Leg Kick Walks
    Knee Ups (Stork Walk)
    Back Kick Step (when stepping back)
    Hoe Downs

Part Three: Pacewalk Routine

Speedwork routines (without weights) Using rapid leg motion and bent arm pumping, sprintwalk in place as fast as you can for one minute, using shuffle steps and the 6-second count method to monitor your speed. Practice low kick walks if you can't go fast enough. Continue for the next minute at your fast walk speed.

Beginners: Go from 70 steps per minute (spm) to 120 spm.
Advanced: Go from 90 to 140 spm in the first five minutes, increasing your speed each minute by 10 spm.

Speed		*SPM*
Brisk Walk	One Minute	100-120
Fast Walk	One Minute	110-130
Sprintwalk	One Minute	120-140
Fast Walk	One Minute	110-130
Brisk Walk	One Minute	100-120

Part Four: Weightwalk Calisthenic Routine

This routine includes four sets of one minute each with 12 to 20 repetitions at the rate of 80 to 100 steps per minute. Use hand-held weights (beginners not more than one to two pound hand and leg weights). Practice this series of leg and arm swings with increasing range of movement. Combine bent arm pumps with higher leg lifts. Next do arm curls and weighted ankle extensions while walking or marching in place.

Repeat the routine using the Three Step routine with arm and leg weights.

Minute One: Walk and Shoulder Presses *Front Press:* Starting with weights at chest level, press up from chest to over the head and let down slowly, keeping both arms in front of your face. Repeat for 12 to 20 counts.

Middle Press: Starting with weights by the side of your ears, press and raise up so arms are straight up behind ears. Repeat for 12 to 20 counts.

Minute Two: Walk and Arm Raises *Side Arm Shoulder Raises:* With hand-held weights hanging at your side, lift arms straight up to shoulder height and lower (do not drop) back down. Repeat for 12 to 20 counts.

Front Arm Chest Raises: With hand-held weights, extend arms in front of you. Alternate left and right arm raises while lifting, simultaneously, the opposite leg, bringing knee waist high. Repeat for 12 to 20 counts.

Breast Beaters: Starting with hand-held weight at chest, extend arms back to the count of two steps and bring arm to your chest for another two counts. Repeat for 12 to 20 counts.

Minute Three: Walk and Curl *Bicep Curl:* With the same side arm and leg, while marching and curling, lift hand weights as you lift the knee waist high. Repeat for 12 to 20 counts.

Tricep Extensions: From the 90-degree Hoe Down position, arms bent 90 degrees and upper arms parallel with the body, extend arms back and straighten as torso bends up and down. Repeat for 12 to 20 counts.

Minute Four: Leg Work with Ankle Weights *Front Leg Extensions:* Bend knee and lift waist high. From this position, straighten leg and return it slowly to bent knee position. Lower leg and repeat movement with other leg. Repeat 6 to 10 counts for each leg.

Back Leg Extension: Back step in place, raising your foot knee high and stepping down again. Alternate legs and repeat for 6 to 10 counts on each leg.

Crossover Legs: Take three crossover steps left, then three right. Repeat for 10 to 20 counts.

Heel Toe Walk: Rolling from heel to toe, raise heel and hold for two counts, then lower it. Repeat for 12 to 20 counts.

Camel Squats: With hand-held weights resting on your shoulders and elbows pointed directly to the side with knuckles facing out, camel walk by bending instead of straightening each leg as it lands, letting your body sink down with each step. Repeat for 6 to 10 counts on each leg.

Part Five: The Climb

Use a step bench, the Stairmaster (see Appendix p. 204), or
nearby stairs for this portion.

Minute One: One Step Up

Step up right, step up left.
Step back down left, back step down right.
Step back down right, back step down left.

Repeat this series: beginners, 10 times; advanced, 15 times.

Minute Two: Two Steps Down

Step up left, step up right.
Step back down left, step back down right.

Repeat this series: beginners, 10 steps up and down;
advanced, 20 steps up and down.

Minute Three: Four Steps Up and Down

Step up right, step up left.
Step up right, step up left.
Step back down right, step back down left.
Step back down right, step back down left.

Beginners repeat 5 up and downs; advanced, 10 up and downs.

Note: If you only have a step bench, repeat exercise done in Minute One.

Crossovers Up and Down *Right crossovers:* With your left side turned nearest the step, cross your right leg over and step up, then return to starting place. Repeat the right crossover step for 5 to 10 counts. *Left Crossovers:* With your right side nearest the step, do left crossover step up. Let your right leg dangle, bring it up and return it to the original position. Repeat for 5 to 10 counts.

Two Steps Up and Down

Up:
Left crossover steps, right side step.
Left crossover steps, right side step.

Down:
(Turn and walk facing down.)

Right crossover step, left side step.
Right crossover step, left side step.
Switch to left crossover steps going up and right crossover steps going down.

Note: If you are doing these on a regular set of stairs, there may not be room for both feet on one step to do crossovers.

Four Steps Up and Down Repeat left-right crossover series with four steps up and down. Beginners, 10 up and down; advanced, 20 up and down.

Dancewalk Cool-Down

It is important not to skip this portion of the Dancewalk Workout. Slow down your pace and do a series of cool-down stretches. Use slow music (perhaps the same as you used for the warm-up section) for this portion of your Workout.

Basic Dancewalk Cool-Down Stretches

1. Hang Over Stretch (p. 56)

2. Inverted V (p. 57)

3. Hip and Back Relaxer (p. 59)

4. Seated Groin and Lower Back Stretch (p. 60)

5. Overhead Leg Stretch (p. 62)

6. Lying Down Neck Stretch (p. 63)

7. Elevating Feet (p. 63)

Make the Dancewalk your creative walk, adding arm, torso, and leg combinations which fit the mood of the music and your own mood. Remember that you can use portions of the Dancewalk Workout as substitutes for any jumping, running or jogging portions of your favorite exercise routine.

Part Three

PERSONALIZED
WALKING

PROGRAMS

1 Customizing Your Workouts

THERE ARE MANY ways to substitute, complement, or supplement your current exercise program with the Walking Workouts to suit your age, sex, and particular sports preference.

Walking for the Over Fifty

If you are over fifty and out of shape or have never exercised seriously, begin slowly. Stop when you are tired and begin again after you have rested. This stop and go method is a slower version of the interval training described in the Pacewalk Workout. If you feel dizzy or nauseous, stop and rest. If the dizziness or nausea persists, check with your doctor.

Before starting your walking program, give yourself a walking distance test. See how far and how long you can walk before getting tired. Try a hundred yards, for example; if that is comfortable, then go another hundred, and so forth. Take 60% of the distance you walked before getting tired and use this as your per-session mileage distance. If you don't feel tired the next day, and no muscles hurt, you probably have the right walking mileage upon which to build. It's usually about an eighth of a mile, more or less, if you are "unexercized." If you are in fit physical condition, begin right in practicing the Pacewalk Workout at the advanced level.

As you do your Workouts, pay particular attention to the stretches and be sure you give equal time to your Daily Walking program, increasing walking time and distance as you can. Many older walkers I know average between five and ten miles a day. They use walking to explore the out of doors as well as museums, atriums, and malls.

Older women (more than older men)

should make an extra effort to walk more. Among the 65-and-older age group, men constitute a disproportionate 75% of those who walk regularly (two to three times a week). After menopause women lose bone mass more rapidly. The Walking Workouts will strengthen the bones along with the muscles, skin, and heart.

Walking for Women

The Walking Workouts are non-sexist. Men and women practice them at equal levels with one exception—weight training. Women's weight loading schedule is different from men's. Otherwise, speed, number of miles and stairs climbed are all the same.

Walking for Children

The Walking Workouts are generally safe for children of all ages, except that the Weightwalk and the Level IV and V intensities should be modified for children under 12. They should do the Weightwalk without weights or with one-pound handheld weights at most. Children under high school age should remain at Level III, and all children should practice the Workouts with adult supervision.

Walking for Runners

If you are a runner, the Walking Workouts will develop and strengthen your leg muscles in a more balanced way than running, skating, bicycling, or aerobic exercises. Walking will help you avoid shin splints and hamstring pulls. World class runner Gayle Olinekova recommends walking in her running program for extra leg strengthening and toning. If you need to cut your jogging miles down to minimize running injuries, you can burn additional calories by walking. Walking and running burn about the same amount of calories per mile, and it's easy to integrate walking into your daily routine by walking to work or walking during your lunch break. If you can arrange to take 10-minute walk breaks during the work day, you will find they help relieve stress and curb the appetite.

It is also a good idea to walk *after* you run. Not only does walking cool you down and stretch you out, it also relaxes you after your high intensity running exercise.

Finally, if your running injuries force you to become a full-time exercisewalker, you will soon discover that life's not so bad in the slow lane. There are walking equivalents of many running movements. The walking version of jogging in place, for example, is marching in place or walking in place with high leg lifts. The walking equivalent of running is the sprintwalk with rapid leg movements and wider steps. Remember, when you are doing the walking version of the exercise, you always have to keep one foot on the ground. Best of all, the Weightwalking at Level IV and V will keep you as aerobically fit as running, and the Climbwalk Workout will probably increase your fitness level. Both these Walking Workouts will give you more upper body exercise.

Walking for Bicyclists

Although bicycling, including exercise cycles, is not jolting to the back and joints, the knee may bend too much for many during the exercise. Walking Workouts do not require as much knee bending. If you bicycle for exercise, alternate a Walking Workout with your bicycle workout for variety in maintaining your aerobic fitness. Split your bicycle workout in half and instead of the second half, do a Pacewalk or Climbwalk Workout. In this way, you'll be exercising a different set of muscles and working your upper body more, toning and strengthening your chest, shoulders, and arm muscles. Any of the four Walking Workouts will combine well with bicycling and will balance the bicyclist's overdeveloped quadricep muscles. If you are at an average fitness level, practice the Workouts at Level III. If you are above average, try the Level IV intensity. Emphasize the Weightwalk calisthenics for upper body work.

If bicycling is a recreational activity for you, substitute bicycling for your Daily Walking, making bicycling your calorie burner and Walking Workouts your aerobic and muscle conditioner. For a change of scenery when you are on a bicycle trip, park, secure your bike, and take a walk up a mountain or into a wilderness area where there are no bicycle routes.

Walking for Dancers

If you practice aerobics or aerobic dancing, there are walking movements to replace the injurious jumping and running movements of many aerobic and calisthenic routines. By using these movements, you will reduce the injury rate of your exercise. I designed the Dancewalk Workout to take the injury out of the aerobic routine. Dancers can substitute the Dancewalk Workout for jogging in place, or practice

the outdoor versions of the Pacewalk, Weightwalk, and Climbwalk Workouts. If you have been doing aerobic dancing on a regular basis, you are probably at a high level of aerobic fitness, and the Weightwalk Level IV will be the best Workout for you. You should also try Pacewalking with a weight loaded backpack.

Walking for Body Builders and Strength Athletes

Walking Workouts provides the best non-injurious aerobic system for practitioners of strength building sports (weight lifters, wrestlers, football players, gymnasts) who do not otherwise get enough aerobic training. The Workouts permit a vigorous, slow, non-jolting exercise, and they allow for weight loading, which strengthens and tones the skeletal muscles while working the heart-lung system.

If you are a body builder or some other type of strength athlete, you already have a lot of upper body and overall muscle strength, so the calisthenic portion of the Weightwalk Workout is probably too light-weight for you. I recommend you skip the calisthenic part and incorporate only its arm and leg movements into the aerobic routine.

Strength athletes complain that jogging hurts their joints and that too much of it reduces their muscle mass. That's the main reason the Weightwalk Workout (minus the calisthenic portion) should be your number one workout. It's better for you than jogging. It cuts down on your aerobic training time, while keeping your muscles, especially your upper body muscles, working along with your heart. Football players, gymnasts, and other strength athletes do not get enough cardiovascular conditioning from their favorite sport no matter how often they practice it. I recommend that all strength athletes do the Weightwalk or Climbwalk Workout, or both, at Level III.

To help you incorporate the Walking Workouts into your regular health club or other weight training routine I recommend this schedule:

Practice the Walking Workout warm-up (for the Pacewalk, Weightwalk or Climbwalk), then do the stretching portion of the Workout or your usual stretching routines. Now, instead of doing the techniques and calisthenics, practice your own weight training routines. After you have completed these, practice Level III of the Weightwalk, Climbwalk, or Pacewalk aerobic routines, the cool-down walk, and light stretching. You should be able to fit all this into about 60 minutes, or maybe a little more. This way, you don't have to have two separate workout programs.

Walking for Racquet Sports Players

Elbow and knee joint pain are often a problem to racquet sports players because these joints are stressed laterally, in a direction they are not meant to go. Unlike jogging, the Walking Workouts will not further stress these aching joints; instead, the Workouts provide a pain-free aerobic exercise.

If you are a recreational racquet sports player, you probably can't play often enough or hard enough each week to make your sport your primary exercise. Walking Workouts give you a way to supplement your play, or to pick up the slack off-season. Working toward and maintaining Level

III should be enough for the recreational racquet sports player. Practice the Pacewalk aerobic routine on the move, or add moderate walking to your exercise program.

Walking for Swimmers

While swimming is a safe, all-around exercise, it is hard to make it a primary one. Places to swim are often expensive and inaccessible. Swimming laps can be boring. You can add variety by splitting your exercise time between walking and swimming. Walking will keep you injury free out of the water and let you visit with friends and family while exercising. (It's hard to talk while blowing air under water.) In addition, walking will help burn off the residue fat that swimming hasn't completely taken care of. A swimmer's body tends to have more fat than other athletes', because the fat acts as an insulation when water is below body temperature.

If you swim for recreation, I recommend you make walking your workout. If you work out with swimming two or three times a week, substitute Walking Workouts for one or two of these, or for half the workout session, using the warm-up walk, stretching, techniques, and cool-down before and after a 30-minute aerobic swimming session. All four Walking Workouts can be substituted for a swimming workout by doing them at an equivalent intensity level, usually III or IV

Walking for Skiers and Mountain Climbers

Mountain hikes have long been considered leg strengthening exercise for both skiers and mountain climbers. When the first women to climb Anapurna trained, they found that while running strengthened their heart-lung system, it did not do enough for leg strength, so they switched to hiking with a backpack.

Now skiers can train their hearts in the off-season by jolt-free brisk walking instead of running. The upper body arm pumping also simulates the poling action of the cross-country skier, strengthening the arms and shoulders.

The Weightwalk and Climbwalk Workouts are probably the best training for downhill skiing, because they will give you more leg strength. The Pacewalk and Weightwalk Workouts complement cross-country skiing because they strengthen the arms. For nordic and alpine skiers, all four Walking Workouts should be the primary off-season exercise.

The Workout Group

ANY GROUP WITH a common interest in health, fitness and walking can become a Walking Workout group. A family workout at a holiday gathering such as Thanksgiving or Christmas would be welcomed when everyone is looking for something to do to burn off the extra calories of the "big dinner." A family workout session can be a time when the whole family gets together for any other social or business reasons as well.

Other natural groups you can organize for Walking Workouts include the members of your health or sports club, senior citizens, ex-smokers, members of Alcoholics Anonymous, dieting groups such as Weight Watchers, YMCA members, singles' club participants, and aerobic dancers. To organize your fellow workers into a walking group try to get the backing of your corporate health and fitness director or the corporate physician. (Doctors are walking's best friends—they prescribe it all the time.) Keeping

employees healthy is in the best interests of the corporation, and walking is a lot cheaper than a multi-million-dollar exercise facility.

Most high school coaches now use running for aerobic training. I hope this book will help them switch to walking. Sports like wrestling, tennis, and baseball lend themselves more easily to Walking Workouts for training than team sports like basketball and football which traditionally rely on running for training. Activities in which walking can become a natural part of a routine such as marching bands, cheerleading, and track and field events will also be more receptive to the Walking Workouts program.

Youth groups such as the Boy Scouts and Girl Scouts can easily adopt Walking Workouts as part of their activity programs and use them to help train for special events such as mountain climbs and canoe trips.

Walking and Hiking Clubs

Established walking and hiking clubs are another good place to introduce Walking Workouts. These clubs vary in their level of interest in walking as exercise. Back-packers have traditionally been more interested in the great outdoors, survival in the wilderness, nature study, and trail building and maintenance than walking for exercise. Hikers have tended to view walking as the "easy" version of hiking. Now that walking's biomechanics are better understood, hiking has, in fact, become an important branch of walking. Hikers are learning that they can become stronger and increase their fitness levels by practicing the Walking Workouts and making them part of their outings. (See p. 194 for more information on hiking organizations.)

Taking It Outside

Practicing the Workouts Outside

Don't confuse the Walking Workouts with your Daily Walking routine. While they are both exercise, one is much more concentrated than the other. You can't get the same amount of exercise from your Daily Walking as you can from the dynamic Walking Workouts. For example, hiking over rugged terrain makes you lift your legs in a way that is similar to the leg lifts you do when marching in place. But your legs usually don't go as high or high as often. To make hiking more dynamic, you need to practice the Weightwalk Workout or the Climbwalk Workout during the hike. These two Workout routines, (unlike the Pacewalk) adapt well to rugged terrain because the speed of movement is not as great.

Similarly, you should distinguish between taking a backpacking trip for fun and doing the Weightwalking Workout in a mountainous area, using a backpack, or hand-held or ankle weights. Remember, it is not really a Walking Workout unless you organize the time and place for a Workout and follow the prescribed training schedule.

Taking the Walking Workouts outside is serious business. Monitor your pulse to see how hard you are working. On a longer hike you need not practice the Workout portion the whole time. You can convert backpacking at a 2-mile-per-hour pace into a weight loading routine by speeding up the pace or loading up with additional weight such as rocks or sand. Try to avoid working so hard on a long backpacking trip that you run out of steam too early.

Daily Mileage

Consider your Walking Workouts program practiced three or four times a week as the core of your aerobic training and body strengthening program. This is all the physical conditioning you need to build and to maintain your basic fitness, but it may not be enough to maintain weight control. Your Walking Workouts will burn from 300 to 1,000 calories per session. While you are still at a low conditioning level, your ability to work hard and therefore burn high numbers of calories will be low, so you should supplement your Workout with Daily Walking of moderate intensity (three miles per hour), trying to walk two to three miles per day. If it's more convenient, you can break these miles up into morning, noon, and evening walks.

Hiking and Backpacking

Weekend hiking and backpacking are walking activities that take you out of the city, into the countryside and wilderness areas. There are a number of regional, national, and international organizations for hikers and backpackers. The Sierra Club organizes weekend hikes as well as outing vacations which include hiking. In the eastern United States, the Appalachian Mountain Club (AMC) arranges overnight hikes. The AMC has chapters stretching from Boston to New York, and publishes walking guides to country walks near major cities. Another major hiking organization is the Appalachian Trail Conference which concentrates on maintaining trails in conjunction with smaller hiking clubs and serves as a clearing house for locating local hiking clubs.

Hiking and Backpacking Organizations

Appalachian Mountain Club
5 Joy Street
Boston, MA 02108

Appalachian Trail Conference
P.O.Box 236
Harper's Ferry, W. VA 25425

Sierra Club Outing Department
530 Bush Street
San Francisco, CA 94108
(415) 981-8634

Rambling and Wandering

Perhaps the oldest form of organized walking is the Wanderclub. (The Black Forest Wanderclub—*Schwarzwald Wanderverein*—was founded in 1867.) These clubs were the first to engage in walking "for its own sake." These walkers or "wanderbirds" view walking as a nature experience, a way to discover the outside world. This type of walking is popular throughout mainland Europe, the British Isles, and Scandinavia. The European Rambler's Association stimulated the development of long distance footpaths (the walker's equivalent of super highways), which link up walking trails in various European countries and provide endurance and discovery opportunities that keep the walker off paved roads and in a forest greenbelt as much of the way as possible.

Ramblers' Associations

European Ramblers' Association
Falkertstrasse 70
D-7000 Stuttgart 1
Federal Republic of Germany
Tel: (0711) 29 53 36

Ramblers' Association (British)
1/5 Wandsworth Road
London SW8 2LJ
Tel: (01) 582 6878

Walking Tours

Almost every major tourist destination has guided walking tours. The city of London, for example, holds five a day; San Diego, three a day. Walking tour maps indicating walking times and distances are available from most tourist bureaus.

Perhaps the best walking tour group is Walkabout International. It is a non-profit walking organization that does not want to be called a club because it declines membership and the formalities that go with maintaining a membership organization. Instead, Walkabout International concentrates on the walks themselves, publishing weekly newsletters to let readers know where Walkabout guides are leading walks. The meeting time and place are given as well as the theme and distance of the walk. Walkabout sponsors both brisk and easy walks, combining walking as sightseeing with walking as exercise. Walkabout International, Inc., 835 Fifth Avenue, San Diego, CA 92101. (619) 231-7463. They have chapters in Los Angeles and Phoenix with more on the way.

Inn-to-Inn Touring

In various parts of the world innkeepers have arranged to forward the baggage of touring walkers by van so that the walkers can walk from inn to inn carrying only a light pack. Thus, they can go 12 to 20 miles a day and concentrate on the walking rather than the lugging. Inn-to-inn tours can be made in Scotland's Highlands, in England's Lake District, in Germany's Black Forest, in the Alps of Austria and Switzerland and in the United States in Vermont and Colorado. Write to Active Travel™ Tours, Box K, Gracie Station, New York, N.Y. 10028 and specify destination.

Racewalking

Racewalking is a citizen's sport, accessible to all classes of competitors from high school students to senior citizens. You can test your racewalking speed in racewalks ranging from one to ten miles, and you can test your overall walking endurance in 20 km, 50 km, and 26.2 mile events. The Walkers' Clubs of America hold weekend clinics for fitness racewalkers and organize racewalking competitions. For a list of Walking Clubs or clinics in your area, send an oversized self-addressed stamped envelope to: Walking World Clubs and Clinics, Box K, Gracie Station, New York, N.Y. 10028.

Dutch Sportwalking

Volksmarching or people's walking are organized walking events which originated in Holland seventy-five years ago as military training or marching exercises and evolved into a sporting event known as four-day marches. Today these international walking events can be found in four- and two-day versions in Japan, Israel, Wales, Vienna, Ireland, Switzerland, and Denmark. Racewalking and running are prohibited at these events for they are not really races; everybody who finishes the distance is a winner. Walkers go at their own pace on circular routes ranging from 10 to 31 miles per day, four days in a row. The length of the route is determined by sex and age: 18- to 34-year-old men must do the 31-mile or 50-km route to qualify for the medal. Women and children can walk shorter distances. Write to International Event Walks, P.O. Box 888, F.D.R. Station, New York, N.Y. 10022 for more information.

German Volksmarching

In 1976 a walking club system in Germany was founded as a protest against running races which were thought to be too professional and exclusionary. The volkssport system was founded to hold sporting events where, like their Dutch counterparts, everyone who finished would be a winner. Today the International Volkssport Association has 6,000 chapters and lists 10,000 annual weekend volksmarches in 15 countries. They are so numerous that you can probably catch a "volksmarch" on any weekend anywhere in Europe.

The American Volkssport Association (AVA) organizes self-paced weekend walks from 6 to 26 miles and certifies walker's mileage. AVA also has a system for recording annual and even lifetime walking mileages. They have 300 chapters in the United States and 4,000 chapters abroad.

Volkssport Associations

The International Volkssport Verein (Association)
1VV-Sekretariat, Postfach 1116
D-8950, Kaufbeuren 1
Federal Republic of Germany

American Volkssport Association (AVA)
National Office, Suite #203
Phoenix Square
1001 Pat Booker Road
Universal City, TX 78148
(512) 659-2112

How to Use Walking to Change Bad Habits

THE WALKING EXERCISE philosophy is one of balance. It's the so-called reasonable man's approach, and it involves self-discipline, self-control, and will power. Mastering a Workout program is in many ways taking control of your life. If you don't succeed the first time you try a workout routine, you can keep working at it. If you succeed for a little while, then slip, you can get back on the track and keep working on it.

The best balanced exercise philosophy is one that acknowledges our weaknesses and propensity to "cheat" but has a built-in system of "patience" that keeps bringing us back on track. Walking as an exercise provides this system and helps you turn bad habits into good ones.

with cigarettes in their mouths. Clearly, walking itself cannot make you stop smoking, but common sense will tell you that it is hard to maintain a smoking habit during vigorous cardiovascular exercise. You cannot breathe heavily and smoke at the same time. Still, some people, once they come to a full stop light up again. A walking habit can substitute for the smoking habit. When you feel the need for a cigarette, take a brief, brisk walk instead (about five to ten minutes). You don't have to go outdoors; fresh air can help, but even a walk indoors, around the office, will stimulate your blood circulation and make you more alert. Walking also helps relieve tension.

Smoking

Statistics show that there are as many smokers in the exercising population as in the non-exercising population. I have seen walkers participating in walking events

Alcohol

Many people don't realize that alcohol contains calories. Don't use it to quench your thirst! Drink water before drinking alcohol, especially after you have exercised.

Meet people for a walk rather than a drink. Many social meetings can take place while walking, and "walking" meetings are often more stimulating than those in a crowded bar or restaurant.

Eating and Overeating

I am often asked what to eat for walking. My shortest answer is, "A nutritionally balanced diet." Exercise burns calories and suppresses the appetite, but it does not give you a license to eat whatever and whenever you want. If you are overweight, use a combination of Walking Workouts and Daily Walking to reduce your weight. Walking will help substitute fat with muscle mass.

Walking and the Walking Workouts can help you control your appetite. Substitute a walk for extra food or snacks and use walking instead of eating in response to stressful situations.

Break up your walking into 10 to 15 minute segments performed when you are most likely to be hungry. Substitute a walk break for a snack break. The principle is exactly the same whether you want to stop smoking, to stop drinking, to stop eating: substitute a good habit (walking) for the bad one. Marching in place, in the "box step" (see p. 92) or in a small office works just as well as a long walk outdoors. The point is to just get up and walk!

Common Questions About Walking

I RECEIVE THOUSANDS OF questions regarding walking as exercise. Here are answers to some of the most frequently asked:

How much exercise is enough?

This depends on your fitness goal. Everyone should strive for good fitness. This is Level III on the Workout charts. Three to four hours a week of Walking Workouts, plus two to four miles of regular walking on non-Workout days will probably be enough time and mileage to maintain yourself at Level III. If you want more exercise for muscle toning and definition, or higher calorie burning, you will need to devote more time and energy, that is, raise the intensity level of your Workouts.

How fast can I walk for maximum aerobic efficiency without having to racewalk?

Most people really can't walk faster than 5.5 mph—about an 11-minute mile

or 150 steps per minute. To exercise harder, you have to add weight; first to your back-pack, then to your hands and ankles. Or you can do stair climbing. For the highest intensity workout, you can combine speed, weight loading, and stair climbing (see p. 153).

Will a lot of walking hurt my flat feet or give me any other medical problems?

I have never heard of any medical problems originating with walking. The walking in *Walking Workouts* is more strenuous than regular walking and includes weight training so you may have to be careful to do more stretching and to increase the intensity of your weight loads very gradually. "Train, don't sprain" is the new exercise philosophy. Proper footwear (good running or aerobic shoes) is essential.

Flat feet, heel spurs, bunions, and even bad knees are problems that can be aggravated by walking, but are not caused by it. Usually their causes are ill-fitting shoes, a family history of the disease, or poor health habits. If you have bad knees, for example, you may find Weightwalking painful because of the additional weight on the bad knee. The Climbwalk Workout may be painful because the knee may bend too much as you step up. You will have to experiment a little to find which Walking Workout will least aggravate your existing problem or injury. Remember, though, that even the Climbwalk Workout requires less knee bending than bicycling and certainly less knee pounding than running. See a doctor before beginning any Walking Workout if you do have a problem or past injury.

Is walking backwards uphill beneficial?

Yes. Changing your walking direction works different muscles. If you are doing a great deal of stair or hill work, for example, be sure to walk *down,* too. Backwards walking up stairs, inclines, and on flat ground will train the leg muscles opposite those trained while walking frontwards. *Walking Workouts* shows you how to become a multidimensional and multidirectional walker.

What's the best time of day to exercise?

It depends on how you live and work. I find I am more energetic and can put more into a Workout in the morning, so I schedule a vigorous Workout in the morning and save my regular walking for the end of the day as a form of relaxation. But some people discover that if they work too hard in the morning, they become fatigued for the work day. A midday Workout is the answer for some. You will have to experiment to find the time that is best for you, but it should never be within two hours after a meal.

Can I exercise while walking with my dog?

Minimally, walking your dog gives you the opportunity to take from two to four walk breaks a day. How do you walk your dog and exercise too? A stroller's pace is certainly fine, but a Pacewalker's pace is much better. Use a longer leash so your dog can be further out in front of you. In this way, you can take the wider strides of the Pacewalk. Tie or fasten the leash to your waist so your arms are free to pump. The faster paced walk will train and condition you without risk to the dog.

Is hiking enough exercise?

Probably not. You would have to do a great deal of hiking to equal a regular Walking Workout, and many hikers and long distance walkers forget to swing their arms, so the upper body conditioning is not as great as it should be. I recommend spending 30 to 60 minutes of your hiking time practicing the Pacewalk, Climbwalk or Weightwalk Workout as your third (or fourth) Workout session of the week. Choose the Workout most appropriate to the terrain (the Pacewalk if the terrain is smooth, the slower-paced Weightwalk or Climbwalk if it is rugged).

Why can't I walk fast enough to get my heart rate into the training zone?

It is usually only after you have reached fitness Level III that you will have problems staying in the aerobic training zone with the fast or Pacewalk. This is because the fitter you become the faster or harder you have to work to maintain your heartbeat in the aerobic training zone. When this happens, practice the sprintwalk routines to increase your speed. After that, carry a weight loaded backpack. If your heart rate is still not up, weight load your hands, then your ankles. Finally, add an incline. Each of these speed and resistance additions should keep you apace with your increasing cardiovascular fitness.

Note: As you begin your Walking Workouts program, you may have questions of your own. Send them to me at Gary Yanker's WALKING WORKOUTS, P.O. Box 888, F.D.R. Station, New York, N.Y. 10022. Keep me posted on your progress or send me any interesting stories for future walking books.

Appendix
Walking Accompaniments

A LONG WITH THE recent explosion of interest in walking as exercise has come a corresponding increase in walking-related items, ranging from walking shoes to high-tech walking equipment. The primary appeal of walking is, of course, that you can do it any time and any place *without* special equipment or accessories. This section is provided for those of you who want to know what's available.

Shoes

Lightweight comfortable footwear that provides support, cushioning, and flexibility is best for working out. Many prefer their running, training, or aerobic dancing shoes, but now there is also the option of special walking shoes. Here's how to see if a pair of shoes will be good for walking:

1. The toe box or toe area should be roomy enough to allow your toes to spread out.

2. The foot bed of the shoe (inside sole) should have adequate cushioning and arch support.

3. The shoe should be flexible and bend where your forefoot bends.

4. The shoe should be cut below the ankle for maximum ankle flexibility; lightweight hiking boots, rather than heavy duty ones, are best for practicing Walking Workouts out of doors.

5. The shoe should have a heel cup which holds your heel in place and reduces side-to-side movement in the shoe.

6. The shoe should allow your foot to breathe. Lining materials that make your foot sweat are not recommended. (It's important to keep your feet as dry as possible to prevent blistering.)

Measuring Devices

A pedometer and a watch are the best devices for measuring walking speed and distance. Electronic watches are now available with built-in pedometers. Some watches also monitor your rate of exercise and number of calories burned.

Treadmills

With a treadmill you can walk fast or walk against resistance while staying in the same place. There are a number of treadmills on the market today, ranging in price from $200 to $3,500. The lower priced treadmills are non-motorized and have no slope adjustments. The more expensive ones are motorized and some include computerized exercise monitors. The main difference between a motorized and non-motorized treadmill is that the former allows you to simulate normal walking while, with the latter, you must use your hip and thigh muscles to help move the belt. For the Walking Workouts, the treadmill should be long enough and wide enough for you to be able to take long strides without having to step off the back and to do crossover steps while walking sideways. You should also be able to swing your arms freely without hitting the railings or measuring equipment.

The Stairmaster

The Stairmaster is, perhaps, the ultimate "high-tech" walking exercise machine. With it you can turn walking into a high intensity exercise. It puts stairwork on a par with other high intensity exercises such as running and cross-country skiing. Depending on your body weight, stairwork will enable you to burn in excess of 1,000 calories in an hour, the equivalent of ten to fifteen miles of walking in an hour.

As of this writing, the Stairmaster is primarily sold to health clubs because it costs about $3,000 and requires at least eight feet of ceiling clearance. The relatively high price tag is due to the computer exercise monitoring device. Before starting to exercise with the Stairmaster, you punch in your age (this determines your heart training zone), your weight (this determines calories per minute you will burn), and your exercise goal (determined by the number of floors you plan to walk. The Stairmaster records 16 steps per floor). The computer monitor indicates your METs levels, steps per minute, and pulse rate. The Stairmaster video screen also shows you the number of calories of exercise performed and tells you whether you are exercising in the heart-rate target training zone. At the end of the workout, Stairmaster prints out a cash-registerlike receipt, listing your final workout performance.

Index